Living With Blind Dogs

*A Resource Book and Training Guide
for the Owners of Blind
and Low-Vision Dogs*

Second Edition

Caroline D. Levin RN

 Lantern Publications

Living With Blind Dogs
A Resource Book and Training Guide for the Owners of Blind and Low-Vision Dogs
Second Edition
ISBN 0-9672253-4-5
Library of Congress Control Number: 2003093147

Illustrations and photographs by Caroline D. Levin (except where otherwise noted)

Front cover photographs: (left) Molly and "Boomer" courtesy of Lauren Emery, (center) Dave Rasmussen and "Bubba" by Caroline Levin, (right) neighbor's child and "Bobbie Sue" courtesy of Sher Wardrip

Back cover photographs: Caroline Levin with "Leo" (top) and "Sophie" (bottom) courtesy of Daniel Levin

Lantern Publications
18709 S. Grasle Road
Oregon City, OR 97045-8899
www.petcarebooks.com
503-631-3491

Printed in Canada

⧎•⧏

Disclaimer: While every precaution has been taken in providing accurate and relevant information, the material in this book is published for educational purposes only. The author and publisher are not engaged in providing veterinary advice.

This book is sold without warranty of any kind, either express or implied. The author, photography models, and publisher assume no responsibility for the care and handling of the reader's dog(s). Neither is any liability assumed from damages resulting from the use of this information or suggestions contained herein.

The photographs in this book merely illustrate points made within the accompanying text. Most of the dogs pictured in this book are not blind. (Exceptions have been noted.) In fact, many of the dogs pictured herein represent kennels that *screen diligently* to avoid hereditary vision problems.

This book is dedicated to:

"Blossom," Joe and Elke Garcia,

"Norman," Steve and Annette McDonald,

"Buddy," Kelly Hayes and Robert Cruz

❊•❊

…three very special dogs and their people
who inspired me to write this book.

Acknowledgements

To my family and friends, thank you for for your help…

The photography cast and crew:
My husband, Daniel Levin and our own dogs: Dachshunds, "Alfi" and "Milo"; and Boxers, "Liebschen," "Beeren," and "Sophie."
Dave Rasmussen and Rottweiler, "Bubba"
Jane Wright and Chihuahua, "Carmen"
Pat and Dennis Leis, and Brittany Spaniels, "Sammy" and "Cheyenne"
Natalie Shellans, Timothy Shellans, Natasha Shellans and English Mastiffs, "Columbo" and "Thriller"
Joeanne Butler and Miniature Schnauzers, "Kizzy" and "Tillie"
Milissa Danceur and Shih Tzu, "Leo"
Elaine Resner and Springer Spaniel, "Katie"
Laurie Tuttle and Labrador Retriever, "Molly"
Lois Golik and Shetland Sheepdog, "Tara"
Helga Zink and Papillion, "Rudi" and Shetland Sheepdog, "Kristi"
Renee Howard and Boxer, "Vinnie"
Charlotte "Chuckie" Staughton and Keeshound, "Casey"
Kim Forbragd

Many thanks to the blind-dog owners who have supplied photographs: Bev Barna, Lea Slaton, Kathy Stefanko, Catherine Jamieson, Shari Burghart, John Willmarth, Joyce Carothers, Lauren Emery, Sher Wardrip, Olivia Bravo, Jamie West, Deborah Wiebe, Claudette Trimblay, Angele Fairchild, Pam Lardear, Maggie Buck, Gary Bessette, and Goldens in Cyberspace.

There have also been countless blind-dog owners who have spoken with me over the years. These are the real "experts," without whom this book would not have been possible — too many to list, but all of them appreciated.

I am grateful for all I have learned from Dawn Jecs, my obedience instructor. She possesses a truly brilliant understanding of canine behavior and I am lucky to know her.

I thank my family and friends who continually support me as I plow through these projects. As always, I am grateful to my husband, Daniel, without whom my books would not be possible, and to my editor, Andrea Rotondo Hospidor, for all her hard work.

And finally, I would like to acknowledge Dr. Osamu Igarashi and his wife, Dr. Ritsyo Igarashi for their support and interest in my work.

Contents

About the Author

With a unique combination of professional experiences, Caroline Levin has created the first-ever resource book for the owners of blind dogs. She has compiled helpful hints from hundreds of blind-dog owners in a clear and organized fashion. With this book, she successfully answers the question most commonly asked by the owners of newly diagnosed dogs:

"What do I do now?"

Photo courtesy of Vern Witake

Caroline Levin's experience in eye care began as Charge Nurse of Ophthalmology Surgery at Good Samaritan Hospital, Portland, Oregon. Her career continued as a surgical scrub nurse and office assistant for a prominent ophthalmologist. She educated human patients about ophthalmic diseases and collaborated with various organizations for the blind.

After a decade in nursing, Levin left that field to become the practice manager of an ophthalmic veterinary clinic. Here, she was able to meld her knowledge of ophthalmology with her love of dogs, developing badly needed educational materials for clients. Levin took the opportunity to meet many blind dogs and talk with their owners. Since then, she has written the first two works on this topic: *Living With Blind Dogs* and *Blind Dog Stories*.

As time passed, readers frequently contacted Levin with related questions about canine healthcare. Levin responded by writing *Dogs, Diet, and Disease*, winner of the prestigious Maxwell Award for "Best Healthcare Book 2001," and *Canine Epilepsy*.

Caroline Levin is also an award-winning dog trainer. She has an in-depth understanding of canine behavior and the methods used to successfully train dogs. She shows her dogs in AKC obedience trials and the new sport of musical canine freestyle. Levin is frequently requested as a guest speaker and has written for a variety of publications.

Photo courtesy of Carl Lindemaier

Preface

After a decade working as an ophthalmic nurse, I made a career change to manage a veterinary eye clinic. Being heavily involved in dog sports made this an agreeable move for me. I was able to combine my love of dogs with my knowledge of ophthalmology.

At the veterinary clinic where I worked, we cared for and cured many canine eye problems. There were, however, times when a dog would be diagnosed as irreversibly blind. This was an emotional moment for the dog's owner and tears were often shed.

Time and time again, dog owners wondered how they were going to deal with this problem. It became clear that while there was nothing more that could be done to help the dog's eyesight, there was much more that could be done to help the dog — and his owner!

I realized that both of these individuals needed help adjusting to blindness. The dog needed to learn new skills in order to maintain a good quality of life. And the owner needed help to become a teacher and a cheerleader. He was going to have to help his dog learn these new skills.

As you and your dog make this transition, you may find yourself playing several roles. Sometimes you will be the caregiver to your dog; and sometimes you will require care and teaching yourself. This is why I wrote the book.

My first goal was to help people deal with the sorrow they felt when their dog was diagnosed as blind. My second goal was to provide dog owners with an understanding of the physical conditions that cause blindness. And lastly, I wanted to provide blind dogs with new skills that would allow them to enjoy the fullest, richest life possible.

In the dog fancy, male dogs are usually referred to as exactly that: "dogs." Females are referred to as "bitches." For ease in writing this book, I've chosen to refer to all canines, both male and female, as "dogs" or "he." This does not represent a higher incidence of illness among males. (I have also referred to all owners as "he.")

Since first writing *Living With Blind Dogs*, I've completed several other books about canine diseases and the factors that contribute to them. The knowledge I have gained has influenced and advanced this second edition.

Caroline D. Levin RN

DEALING WITH LOSS

Many people feel a great sense of loss when their dog is diagnosed as blind. Some may feel overwhelmed after simply skimming through the pages of this book. Others may cry, feel anger, or isolation in their grief. Some owners may even consider euthanizing a blind dog. All of these reactions are normal.

There is a sense of helplessness associated with irreversible blindness. As one owner explains it, "There is a distinct type of grief we experience when someone we love goes from being 'whole' to being handicapped."

Some owners are sad for their dog's sake, wondering what quality of life they can expect for their pet. Others are sad for their own sake. They may ask themselves questions such as:

Will I still love my dog as much as I did before the blindness?
Will he be as good as everyone else's dog?
Will my friends and family pity him?
Will my dog be miserable?

Author Elisabeth Kübler-Ross is well known for her work in the area of grief management. She has outlined five stages people typically experience as they cope with loss: Denial, anger, bargaining, depression, and finally, acceptance. This progression can certainly be applied to the dog owner as he adjusts to his dog's new condition.

Grieving is like a roller-coaster ride with many ups and downs. People experience these stages in varying sequences. Some move through one stage, only to return to it at a later time. Other people may even employ more than one coping mechanism at the same time.

The way in which an individual copes may depend on the nature of the relationship he has with the dog. Someone closely bonded may experience a tremendous degree of grief. Other recent losses in one's life can compound the intensity of the feeling.

Denial

Initially, a common way to cope with loss is through denial. Denial protects the mind from the bad news being received. A dog owner may seek out a second or third medical opinion, in hopes of hearing that the problem was misdiagnosed or that the dog will experience a miraculous recovery.

When an owner is in denial, the situation may seem unreal to him. He may continue daily activities just as if the dog were not losing vision, even to the point of withholding medical care. During this phase, an owner may distance himself emotionally from his pet. By reducing contact with the dog, the owner can avoid facing his own pain.

Anger

Eventually, denial gives way to anger. This is a time when a dog owner may say to himself, "This is so unfair. Why did this happen to my dog?!"

In normal instances, humans are the caretakers, guardians, and rule-makers for their dogs. At the onset of canine blindness, a dog owner may feel that he is no longer in control of the situation. This may contribute to his level of anger. An inability to ensure a pet's well-being can be enormously frustrating and even frightening.

It is not uncommon for the dog owner to have angry feelings toward the veterinary staff, as well. In the owner's mind, not only did the veterinarian make this diagnosis, but he is also unable to cure the problem!

Anger may also be expressed toward friends and family members, frequently taking the form of criticism in how they care for the dog. It is important to recognize that such outbursts may only be expressions of the owner's grief.

It is even possible for the owner to express anger toward the dog. He doesn't truly blame the dog for becoming blind. He is simply frustrated and wishes he could restore the dog's vision. Happily, dogs are immensely forgiving creatures and may never remember this stage.

Feelings of guilt can be associated with the anger stage. The owner may question his own care of the dog and wonder if something he did could have caused the vision loss. Such guilt may manifest itself in a number of unhealthy ways. One example is excessive coddling of the dog.

Bargaining

The anger stage is sometimes followed by a bargaining stage. An owner may believe at some level that if denial and anger did not resolve this problem, he may be able to negotiate or bargain for a cure.

The bargaining is usually done secretly, with a Higher Power. One example might be: "If you give my dog his sight back, I will never raise my voice to him again!" Bargaining is a way to keep hope alive. This phase is often short-lived and the dog owner may progress to a state of depression.

Depression

Depression, or sorrow, may set in when the signs of vision loss can no longer be denied. Some owners mistakenly believe that blindness may be a death sentence or, at least, a major disability for their dog. They believe that their most enjoyable activities — such as hiking in the woods or running together on the beach — will be lost.

While friends might try to cheer the grieving owner, it is important to allow the transition through this stage. It's essential for each owner to give himself permission to grieve. Sorrow is actually a healing emotion. It allows one to prepare for the future and accept the realities of living with a blind dog.

Photo of blind Greyhound, "Boomer," courtesy of Lauren Emery

The time it takes for a person to move through this stage can vary greatly. There is no predetermined timetable. Eventually, the feelings of sadness and helplessness will give way to feelings of acceptance: The final stage.

Acceptance

Acceptance is reached when an individual has had time to work through all the previous stages. There is no average time for this process. As one dog owner puts it, "It takes as long as it takes." Talking with sympathetic friends and enjoying the smallest of pleasures with your dog may help.

Once an owner is no longer isolated or in denial, no longer angry or depressed, he reaches a stage of resolution. Now he becomes less of a patient himself and more of a caregiver to his dog. It is at this point that healthcare information is best received.

If an owner has not really reached the acceptance stage, he may have negative reactions to caring for his dog. He may have difficulty remembering instructions. This is an important concept for both veterinary staff and the owners of newly diagnosed dogs.

As the acceptance stage is reached, it is valuable to consider this question: What are the *jobs* dogs do in this day and age?

With the exception of a few dogs that truly earn their keep as herding dogs, hunting dogs, or service dogs, most dogs today are generally unemployed. Our dogs have only a few basic functions in our homes. They alert us to visitors at the door. They want to cuddle in one form or another. And, they make us laugh.

Blind dogs can do all these things as well as other dogs.

While blindness will certainly have an effect on your dog, it is important to remember that you will both be able to maintain many activities of daily living and recreation. This book will give you the information and confidence to help you and your dog return to a sense of being "whole." You will regain a sense of control over your dog's health. With time, living with canine blindness will simply become part of your daily routine.

It is easy to think that you must be an instant expert — that you must know so many things at once. Learning about dog training and healthcare is more like a journey. Each day you will understand more about how your dog reacts and adapts. Turn to sections in the book that are most pressing to you now and read other sections as your schedule permits. Dealing with one thing at a time will help keep it all manageable.

As you progress with your dog's training, you may find yourselves bonding more closely. Helping your dog adjust tends to deepen trust and improve communication. There is a special relationship that develops when you care for a dog with special needs.

Children and Loss

Try to include children in the grieving process. Children often share a very strong bond to the family pet. Vision loss can be especially frightening to them. They may experience feelings of anger and worry.

Including children in these painful times teaches them several things: That it is good to express emotion, how to develop coping skills, and how to learn consideration for others. As with yourself, give children permission to grieve.

Photo of blind Chihuahua, "Bobbie Sue," courtesy of Sher Wardrip

Children can obviously sense when something is wrong. Avoiding the issue or lying about the dog's condition could result in lack of trust or irrational fear on the child's part. Adults who show respect for children's feelings help them build confidence in dealing with loss.

Openness and honesty encourage questions from the child. Straightforward answers are the best tactic. Be patient, as children may need to revisit issues repeatedly. Whenever appropriate, try to include all family members in the process of dog training. Teach them how to behave around a blind dog.

References

Kübler-Ross, E., *On Death and Dying: What the Dying Have to Teach Doctors, Nurses, Clergy, and Their Own Families.* New York: Touchstone Books, 1969.

Ross, C.B., and Baron-Sorensen, J., *Veterinarian's Guide to Counseling Grieving Clients.* Lenexa: Veterinary Medicine Publishing Company, 1994.

ANATOMY OF THE EYE

Many blind-dog owners are not quite certain about the details of their dog's condition. When asked about their dog's blindness, they may respond, "I was so confused by what the doctor was saying," and "I really didn't understand it all."

As with human illnesses, the shock of the diagnosis may hamper your initial ability to comprehend the information. You may not process what you hear, or you may quickly forget it. Healthcare professionals estimate that clients forget about eighty percent of the information they receive in a doctor's office. In addition, the doctor may be uncomfortable delivering the news, and may not make himself clearly understood. The next two chapters will remedy this situation.

However, before we can discuss the causes of blindness, an understanding of the canine eye is necessary. This chapter will outline some of the normal anatomy (structure) and physiology (function) of the canine eye. This knowledge will assist in the understanding of your dog's condition and behavior.

NOTE: The following illustrations are designed to permit easy viewing of the various ophthalmic structures. These drawings do not represent true anatomical proportions.

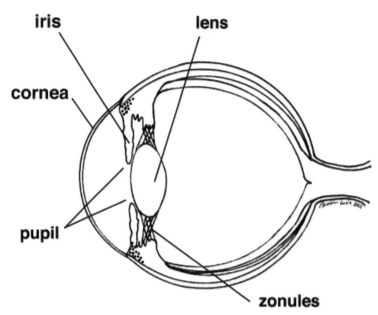

The Cornea (KOR-nee-ah)

The front-most structure of the eye is called the cornea. This thin, normally transparent tissue consists of several layers of cells. These cells function to keep the cornea clear and allow light to pass further into the eye. In the canine eye, the cornea is largely responsible for focusing light waves onto the retina (the lining on the back of the eye). This helps provide clear images to the brain.

The Iris and the Pupil

Located behind the cornea is the iris. This is the colored portion of the eye; the structure gives your dog blue or brown eyes. It has the ability to constrict in bright light in order to shade the interior of the eye. To aid vision, the iris can dilate in dim light, thereby permitting all possible light to enter into the eye.

The opening in the center of the iris is called the pupil. It appears as a black dot because observers are actually looking into the back portion of the eye, which is dark.

The Lens

The lens is located just behind the iris and is held in place by tiny fibers called zonules. The lens is usually clear and shaped like the lens of a magnifying glass (or an M&M's® candy). The lens functions in conjunction with the cornea to focus light upon the retina, or *focus* on objects.

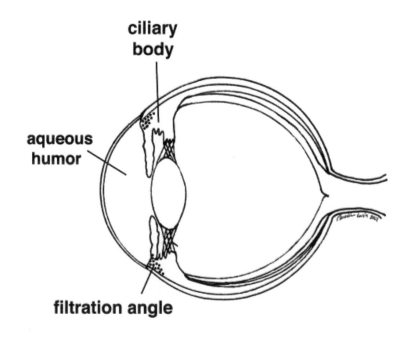

The Aqueous (A-kwee-us) Humor

The area between the cornea and the lens is called the anterior chamber. This chamber is filled with aqueous humor, a fluid that helps nourish the cornea.

The aqueous is produced at the same rate that it exits the eye. Normal canine intraocular pressure (IOP) varies between 15mmHG to 30mmHg. This exchange occurs entirely inside the globe of the eye. It is a separate system from tearing, which occurs on the exterior of the eyeball.

The Ciliary (SILLY-erry) Body and Filtration Angle

The ciliary body is a structure located just behind the iris. It produces aqueous humor. Aqueous exits the eye through a tiny drainage field called the trabecular meshwork or filtration angle. This structure is located between the iris and the cornea, where the iris attaches to the wall of the eye. Since fluid normally drains at approximately the same rate it is produced, this system results in a constant pressure within the eye.

Dog owners and veterinarians report several normal variations in pressure. IOP tends to fluctuate from morning to evening. Owners report pressure spikes during storms (when the surrounding barometric pressure drops) and while driving over mountain ranges (high altitude).

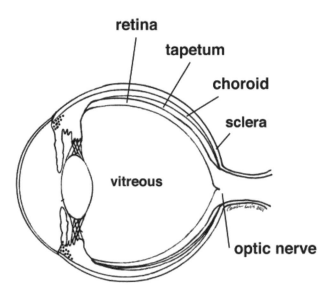

The Retina

Lining the back of the eye is a delicate structure called the retina. The retina is comprised of ten layers, several of which are important to our discussion.

One of the innermost layers consists of ganglion cells. These cells send visual information from the eye, through the optic nerve, and on to the brain. Ganglion cells function very much like nerve cells. They respond to the same neurotransmitters (brain chemicals) that allow nerves to send messages throughout the body.

Deeper within the retina is a layer of specialized photoreceptor cells called rods and cones. They play a considerable role in facilitating vision. When the rods and cones are stimulated by light waves, a chemical reaction is initiated. These chemicals are quickly converted into electrical signals that leave the eye via the optic nerve. This electrical process results in the sensation we know as vision.

Cone cells function predominantly in bright light and assist with fine, detail vision. Cones are also responsible for color discrimination. Based on experiments (objective and subjective), veterinary ophthalmologists believe that dogs *do* have some color vision.

Rods function in low light and detect moving objects. Canine eyes are comprised predominantly of rods. This is a common design among animals that needed to hunt for their food. For hunters, recognizing movement is more important than seeing fine detail.

Just below the layer of rods and cones is the retinal pigment epithelium. This thin layer of cells provides nutrients to the rods and cones.

The Vitreous Body

The area between the lens and the retina is filled with a substance called the vitreous body. It is a jelly-like material that helps the globe maintain shape and form.

The Tapetum (Tah-PEE-dum) Lucidum

The tapetum, not found in human eyes, is located just behind the canine retina. This structure helps reflect and amplify light, which along with numerous rod cells, improves nighttime vision.

The tapetum is responsible for the greenish glow seen when light is shined into the eyes of most dogs. (Some dogs — toy breeds, and blue-eyed dogs — may have a tapetum that is either reduced in size or absent altogether.)

The Choroid (KOE-royd)

Behind the tapetum, the choroid lines the back of the eye. This structure is mainly comprised of blood vessels that feed the retina.

The Sclera

The outermost wall or casing of the eyeball is called the sclera. It is a firm, fibrous tissue that gives the eye form and helps protect the internal structures of the eye.

Now that you understand some basic canine anatomy, we can discuss the common causes of vision loss. Vision loss may be complete or partial, painful or painless, and sometimes associated with other symptoms. An understanding of your dog's condition will help *you* help him.

References

Slatter,D., *Fundamentals of Veterinary Ophthalmology*. Philadelphia: W.B. Saunders Company, 2001.

DISEASES THAT CAUSE BLINDNESS

The veterinary ophthalmologist will perform a number of tests in order to diagnose the degree and cause of vision loss. He will examine your dog's eyes with one or more ophthalmoscopes. These instruments provide a clear view of the internal eye structures, including the lens, drainage angle, and iris. If the dog's lens is clear, the doctor will also be able to examine the vitreous and retina.

A bright light flashed across each eye will assess the pupillary light reflex (PLR). An intact PLR typically indicates that nerve pathways to the brain remain, although vision may be minimal. The menace response (or blink reflex) evaluates the dog's natural reflex to avoid a moving object (the doctors hand). Your dog may also be asked to negotiate an obstacle course.

The veterinary ophthalmologist may recommend that an electroretinogram (ERG) be performed. Much like an electrocardiogram (EKG, the test that measures heart function), an ERG measures the function of the retina. This procedure is performed under general anesthesia. Electrodes are attached around the dog's head and various lights are flashed into the eye. If the retina is functioning normally, a waveform will appear on the computer screen. If the wave is flattened or nonexistent, the retina is not functioning correctly. An ERG is useful in diagnosing cases of retinal diseases and evaluating candidacy for cataract surgery.

If you are trying to evaluate your dog's vision loss at home, be aware that other cues, such as scent and air movement, may contribute to false impressions. One suitable test is to hold a cotton ball waist-high and several feet in front of your dog. Release it and note his ability to follow it.

The following sections discuss some of the reasons that dogs go blind. There are many individual causes of vision loss. The most common causes are discussed here.

Keratoconjunctivitis Sicca (KCS) or Dry Eye Syndrome

Description
As the name implies, KCS results in reduced tear production from the glands surrounding the eye.

Cause
KCS can stem from a number of causes including certain sulfa and anti-inflammatory medications, radiation, normal aging, trauma, surgical removal of the lacrimal (tear-producing) gland, or autoimmune destruction. In the latter, antibodies that have been previously programmed to attack a foreign amino acid chain (such as a virus or dietary protein) mistakenly attack the tear-producing tissues of the eye.

Signs / Symptoms
Common signs include dryness, itchiness, and corneal ulcers. Dog owners sometimes use the term "goopy eyes" to describe the presence of green or light-brown mucous discharge. KCS is frequently misdiagnosed as an eye infection but antibiotic treatment will not resolve the problem.

KCS often occurs in the presence of other autoimmune diseases such as systemic lupus erythematosus (SLE), diabetes mellitus, and thyroiditis.

Prognosis
Lifelong treatment is generally required to avoid painful corneal ulcers, scarring, and progressive vision loss.

Treatment
KCS is commonly treated with cyclosporin drops. Cyclosporin is a medication thought to reduce the immune-mediated reaction. Other medications your veterinarian may prescribe are Optimmune drops or ointment (a milder form of cyclosporin); KCS drops, which often consist of antibiotics; mucomyst (an ingredient that breaks up mucous); and a lubricant. Additional medications may include oral pilocarpine (which stimulates tear production) and non-prescription lubricating drops.

Progressive Retinal Atrophy (PRA) or Degeneration (PRD)

Description

At present, both of the terms PRA and PRD are used to refer to a group of retinal disorders. There are multiple forms of the disease, two of which are responsible for the majority of cases diagnosed. The first is **generalized PRA**, which includes cases of both early onset and late onset. The second form was once called centralized PRA but has now been reclassified as **retinal pigment epithelial degeneration** (RPED). (See page 18.)

In PRA, the cells of the retina gradually deteriorate or atrophy (shrink). Upon examination, the veterinary ophthalmologist can actually see the tapetum — the layer of tissue below the retina — shining through the thinning retinal cells. Over time, vision continues to worsen, hence the term *progressive*. PRA is not a painful condition for the dog.

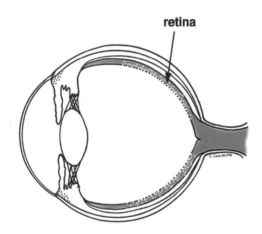

retina

Generalized PRA

Cause

There are some misconceptions about the cause of PRA. This condition is not caused by trauma or the use of whelping-box heat lamps. The cause of generalized PRA is a genetically inherited condition that affects both eyes. In most cases, it is a simple recessive trait.

Signs / Symptoms
PRA can cause the pupils to dilate such that the iris (the colored portion) is barely visible. This dilation represents the body's attempt to supply more light to the retina. As the retinal cells deteriorate, the greenish glow of the tapetum may become more noticeable. In certain instances, cataracts may also develop.

There are two types of generalized PRA. One type occurs early in life. This is called early onset PRA or rod-cone dysplasia (RCD). The term *dysplasia* means that rod and cone cells do not develop correctly. Shortly thereafter, the cells begin to degenerate. The time frame can range from age six weeks to two years. Commonly affected breeds include the Collie, Irish Setter, Miniature Schnauzer, and Norwegian Elkhound.

In other cases, vision loss may not be noticed until the dog is older, at approximately two to six years of age. This type of PRA is called late onset or progressive rod-cone degeneration (PRCD) and is often diagnosed in the American and English Cocker Spaniel, American Eskimo, Belgian Malinois, English Setter, Labrador Retriever, Miniature Poodle, Papillion, Portuguese Water Dog, Rottweiler, and Samoyed.

In cases of generalized PRA, both early and late-onset, many owners first notice a vision loss in low-light situations: Dusk and nighttime. This is because the rod cells are often the first to be affected.

With time, the degeneration will progress to the cone cells, affecting daytime vision, as well. The dog might start bumping into objects or misjudging the height needed to jump onto the couch. He may be reluctant to do things he once did, such as run down a flight of stairs or hop into the car.

Prognosis
Since there are various forms of the disease that can differ between breeds, the progression of PRA can vary widely. However, it will progress to complete vision loss. Some doctors believe that the younger in life a dog is affected, the faster the progression. Typically, a dog will proceed from the first signs of vision loss to the end-stage in about six months to a year.

By the time an owner notices behavioral changes in his dog, the condition is actually fairly well advanced. Some owners may not even notice any problems until the dog is taken to an unfamiliar environment, such as a friend's house. There, the vision loss may become apparent as the dog bumps into obstacles. This is a good example of how dogs can adjust to the slow progression of vision loss in their own surroundings.

In these instances, owners may mistakenly think their dog *suddenly* went blind. But in reality, these dogs have gradually memorized the layout of the yard and home. They have also learned to use other subtle cues such as scents, sounds, and temperature changes in order to navigate. It is only in an unfamiliar environment that the vision loss becomes apparent to the onlooker.

Treatment

In cases of generalized PRA, there is no known cure. Prevention is sometimes considered as one form of treatment for this disease. Prevention means that afflicted animals — or the littermates or parents of an afflicted animal — should not be used for breeding purposes. (Please see Chapter 4, *Genetics and Blindness*, for further discussion.)

If any puppy in the litter is afflicted with PRA, it means some of the other puppies will be carriers of the faulty gene. Without knowing which dog is a carrier and which dog is unaffected, breeding any of the dogs from this litter can reproduce the disease. Annual rechecks with the veterinary ophthalmologist may be recommended in order to evaluate possible cataract development.

Retinal Pigment Epithelial Degeneration (RPED) or Central PRA

Cause

Central PRA has recently been renamed retinal pigment epithelial degeneration (RPED) as this condition is not as closely related to generalized PRA as was once thought. New research suggests that RPED is due to a vitamin E deficiency, which is secondary to a dysfunction of the liver. This condition affects a number of breeds including the Border Collie, Briard, Cocker Spaniel, Rough and Smooth Collie, Golden Retriever, Hungarian Puli, Labrador Retriever, Shetland Sheepdog, and Welsh Corgi.

In RPED, degeneration begins in a thin, pigmented layer of cells that lies beneath the rods and cones. Degeneration of the rods and cones follows. Studies suggest that this damage stems from the body's inability to retain sufficient levels vitamin E in the bloodstream. Researchers believe that this results from a genetically inherited problem involving vitamin E metabolism in the liver.

Vitamin E is an important nutrient for normal retinal and immune system function. Studies indicate that it acts as an antioxidant, protecting the retinal cell membranes from the effects of oxidative stress.

Signs / Symptoms

In cases of RPED, damage is confined to the center of the retina. Age of onset is variable and can range from one to six years, or later. RPED is diagnosed predominantly in working breeds.

Dogs suffering from RPED may lose daylight vision first, unlike dogs with generalized PRA. Owners may realize that their dogs have difficulty locating stationary objects directly in front of them due to the central vision loss. Peripheral vision may still permit them to locate moving objects, such as a rolling ball.

Prognosis

RPED may progress more slowly than generalized PRA and does not always progress to complete blindness. These dogs tend to retain a degree of peripheral vision. Researchers believe that the progression of RPED may be slowed by by supplementation of oral vitamin E.

Treatment

Researchers at the Royal Veterinary College, University of London, recommend supplementing the dog's diet with 600IU to 900IU of natural source vitamin E twice daily with food. Natural source vitamin E is listed as *d*-alpha tocopherol, whereas synthetic forms of vitamin E are listed with the prefix *dl*. The body absorbs natural vitamins more easily than synthetic vitamins.

Supplementing the diet with foods high in vitamin E provides both a natural and complete range of vitamin E molecules. Foods high in vitamin E include green vegetables such as broccoli and leafy greens, plant oils, egg yolks, sardines, almonds, sweet potatoes, winter squash, tomatoes, and peanuts (peanut butter).

It is also recommended that breeds predisposed to RPED should receive routine screening examinations. In this way, retinal changes may be diagnosed in their earliest stages and noticeable vision loss may be prevented.

Sudden, Acquired Retinal Degeneration (SARD)

Description
The first cases of SARD were diagnosed in the 1980s. Like PRA, Sudden, Acquired Retinal Degeneration involves a deterioration of the rods and cones. It is also a bilateral disease (affects both eyes). Unlike PRA, however, the onset of SARD is much different.

Owners of dogs diagnosed with SARD report that their dogs seemed to go blind suddenly or overnight. There is very little warning and little time for the dog to adjust to this sudden change.

SARD frequently affects middle-age females in the age range of six to ten years. It is not limited to specific breeds. This disease usually results in complete and total blindness. While it is not physically painful, many owners report concurrent health problems such as excessive thirst, hunger, weight gain, insomnia, and confusion. These are all symptoms of excess cortisol production. (Cortisol is the body's natural steroid hormone, produced by the adrenal glands, to soothe irritation.)

Causes
While the cause of SARD is still unproven, it is assumed to be a non-genetic condition. Researchers describe the actual mechanism of degeneration as *apoptosis* or programmed cell death.

In humans, a gene called the p53 gene has been identified for its role in destroying damaged or mutated cells in the body. It does this by initiating a self-destruct message, or apoptosis, inside the damaged cell. (This process normally prevents the growth of cancer cells.)

Cellular damage occurs for a variety of reasons including damage to the DNA material or to the membrane, oxidative stress (free radical damage), exposure to radiation, noxious chemicals, or improper nutrition. When the body detects such damage to a cell, the hormone cortisol crosses the cell membrane and initiates the programmed, self-destruct message. Man-made steroids, similar to cortisol, are commonly used by researchers to initiate apoptosis in laboratory studies.

Therefore, we *must* question why dogs produce excess cortisol. The most well-known reason is a tumor of the pituitary or adrenal glands (Cushing's disease). Another reason is chronic stress. This author submits that SARD is triggered by the modern day lifestyle, specifically: Inappropriate **nutrition** plus **chronic irritation** (stress).

Why Nutrition Matters

A closer look at commercial pet food reveals some surprising facts. It may not provide the excellent nutrition advertised. Commercial pet food is highly processed. This damages vitamins, trace minerals, and fatty acids: Nutrients vital for normal retinal health. Even if these nutrients are added back into the food mixture after processing, they are frequently in forms that are difficult for the body to absorb.

Commercial pet foods also contain a wide variety of chemical additives, including BHT, BHA, and ethoxyquin. These industrial preservatives that have been banned from human foods because of links to cancer, autoimmune diseases, and neurological problems.

Frequently, inorganic and toxic dyes are added to commercial food. These artificial colors are some of the most hazardous chemical mixtures added to foods. A large percentage of them have never been tested for adverse affects. Others are documented as toxic to the liver, carcinogenic to thyroid cells, or linked to adrenal gland problems in dogs. Researchers have long-realized that industrial chemicals and damaged nutrients (vitamins, fatty acids, and antioxidants) result in damage to the retina.

Commercial foods contain many other additives, in addition to dyes and preservatives. According to the Animal Protection Institute, pet-food companies are not required to list these chemicals on product labels. Common additives include binding and anti-caking agents, drying agents, texturizers, stabilizers, thickeners, clay products, and flavorings.

One such flavoring is MSG. This additive is classified as an excitotoxin, which damages retinal and other nerve cells. Studies indicate that animals fed MSG produce higher than average levels of cortisol, the stress hormone.

Most commercial pet foods consist mainly of grain products, which are not biologically appropriate for the dog. Grains are receiving more scrutiny for their role in endocrine (hormone) problems. Canine nutritionists explain that dogs are not designed to digest grain and that diets high in grain irritate the gastrointestinal (GI) tract. Chronic, low-grade irritation can cause difficulty in absorbing fat-soluble vitamins and fatty acids.

Additionally, highly processed diets (those that do not contain any fresh foods) place an increased workload on the pancreas. This can lead to pancreatic inflammation and slowed digestion, allowing substantial time for chemicals to further irritate the GI tract. These various sources of inflammation increase cortisol production.

Excess Cortisol Production — Patterns and Effects

Excess cortisol can be damaging in myriad ways. One serious effect is decreased arterial blood flow. This may result in inadequate oxygen delivered to the retina. Excess cortisol is also responsible for cell membrane damage. Consequently, nutrients (glucose) and oxygen have difficulty entering the cell, while waste products have difficulty leaving it.

The concept of stress adaptation is a well-accepted phenomenon. Biologists describe it as an organism's ability to successfully adjust to stressful changes in the environment. This process is marked by three stages: Adaptation, alarm, and exhaustion.

The first stage, **adaptation**, describes the period when short-term irritants or stressors are well managed. Cortisol secretion is appropriately turned on and off by another hormone produced by the pituitary gland called adrenocorticotrophic hormone or ACTH.

Chronic stress, however, can push adrenal gland function into unhealthy, abnormal patterns. Chronic irritation can lead to the **alarm** phase in which the adrenal and pituitary glands may become enlarged from chronic demand. The feedback mechanism located in the brain, which normally shuts off cortisol secretion, becomes damaged. Dogs at this stage become "stuck in overdrive" and exhibit the signs of excess cortisol. Other hormones, such as adrenal estrogen, may also be produced in excess during this phase.

Finally, some individuals may pass from a period of excessive adrenal function to a period of excessively low function. This is the third stage of the stress response known as adrenal **exhaustion**. The glands may produce insufficient levels of cortisol or cortisol that is unable to perform its job at the molecular level. (It is biologically inactive.)

An irritating diet — along with excessive vaccines and harsh pesticides — cause cortisol levels to rise. High levels of cortisol damage cell membranes and prevents the normal transfer of nutrients and oxygen. Cortisol then enters the cells and initiates apoptosis. A tumor (a positive Cushing's diagnosis) *need not be present for adrenal glands to function excessively.*

Studies done in both human and veterinary healthcare indicate that endocrine problems are generally more common in females. The leading theory suggests that the female design may play a large role in these statistics. The female body is designed to carry a fetus — essentially a foreign protein — without attacking it. Consequently, the female body suppresses the normal immune response with an increased ability to secrete cortisol or a greater sensitivity to cortisol and ACTH.

Signs / Symptoms

The retina appears physically normal to the veterinary ophthalmologist at the onset of blindness. It can continue to appear normal until three to four months *after* that time. Signs of excess cortisol frequently accompany the onset of blindness. These include increased appetite, thirst, and urination, weight gain, insomnia, seizures, confusion (circling), muscle weakness (rear leg weakness, incontinence, or cardiac problems), panting, pacing, calcium deposits, skin and coat changes, hearing loss, and lethargy.

Behavioral symptoms of SARDS can be similar to those seen in PRA / PRD, including hesitancy to jump, failure to judge distance, and bumping into objects. High cortisol levels are also known to damage brain-cell function. This can cause symptoms that might be mistaken for behavioral problems such as depression, aggression, fear, and confusion. Owners may become frustrated training SARD dogs. The dog may make poor, slow progress. Excess cortisol hampers these dogs in ways that other blind dogs are not.

Prognosis

Following the initial, sudden onset of blindness, there is little change in the status of the dog's eyes. Over the course of three to four months, the retinal cells will thin out until the greenish glow of the tapetum becomes visible.

In some cases, signs of excess cortisol precede or accompany the vision loss but later dissipate. In other cases, signs of excess cortisol production continue or worsen. This scenario may lead to additional health problems.

Presently, the laboratory tests most commonly performed to evaluate cortisol production are those used to diagnose Cushing's disease — a condition in which a tumor grows on the pituitary or adrenal glands. These tests include the ACTH stimulation test and several dexamethasone suppression tests.

When these blood tests are performed on SARD patients, the results can vary. Sometimes the results come back as "normal," "borderline," or "inconclusive." At other times the tests are positive for Cushing's disease (a tumor). Occasionally, the tests are initially negative, but indicate a tumor at a later date. Therefore, your veterinarian may recommend periodic retesting.

The Cushing's tests are not completely reliable, however. And, in this author's opinion, they are not entirely applicable to the SARD dog. Cushing's tests are designed to identify tumors. SARD dogs may have inconclusive results because they are "stuck in overdrive." That is, they are stuck in the alarm phase of the stress adaptation response. This is a case of high demand on the adrenal and pituitary glands; not tumor growth.

The result may be "normal" or only slightly elevated test results. Glands that function excessively (those in overdrive) will produce high daily levels of cortisol and their related signs and symptoms, but may still respond "normally" to a Cushing's test.

Exhausted adrenal glands produce insufficient levels of cortisol or cortisol that is biologically inactive. Exhausted adrenal glands may also result in a "normal" ACTH stimulation test since they are unable to respond to stress. While some may take such test results to mean that the adrenal glands are in good health, this is far from true. Adrenal exhaustion often results in elevated levels of adrenal estrogen which, in turn, binds with thyroid hormone, even oral thyroid replacement hormone. Additionly, adrenal exhaustion disrupts the immune system. Immunoglobulin levels (such as IgA and IgM) drop. Infection is common. These scenario (high adrenal estrogen, low thyroid and IgA) can be diagnosed via an Immunology and Endocrinology panel by your veterinarian.

Treatment

The veterinary ophthalmologist may recommend that an ERG or electroretinogram be performed. This test will help the doctor discern if the problem involves the brain, optic nerve, or the retina (the latter confirming the diagnosis of SARD).

There are recommended treatments for optic nerve inflammation and for brain cancer. At this time, there is no cure for SARD. However, if cortisol-related symptoms continue or worsen (weight gain, confusion, etc.), or if general health declines, please see the resource book, *Dogs, Diet, and Disease* — page 184 — for various therapeutic options:

For the dog in the alarm phase (adrenal overdrive) — Numerous SARD-dog owners report that the following measures have been effective in reducing the clinical symptoms of excess cortisol: Minimizing or eliminating excessive vaccines and pesticide use; and switching the dog to homemade meals and supplements (Phosphatidyl Serine). While a less-irritating lifestyle may not return visual function, it provides the best chance for improved quality of life, reduced confusion, and a better adjustment to blindness.

For the dog experiencing adrenal exhaustion — When adrenal glands no longer produces sufficient cortisol, hormone replacement therapy is required. Holistic veterinarians recommend dosing these dogs with *low*, physiological levels of cortisol-like steroids. This therapy is also practiced in human healthcare. With treatment, it's common for low thyroid symptoms to abate; and IgA, and adrenal estrogen levels to normalize.

For the dog that develops Cushing's disease — A variety of treatments are currently available to curb cortisol production, minimize it's affects, and reduce tumor growth.

Retinal Dysplasia and Detachment

Description
Retinal dysplasia or retinal folds are both terms used to describe a malformation of the retina. This condition is characterized by folds or puckers in the retinal layers. When the retina is poorly attached to the structures below, it can pull away from the sclera, resulting in retinal detachment and vision loss.

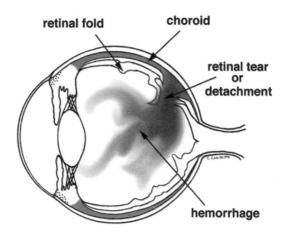

Causes
Retinal dysplasia is a congenital malformation of the retina. It can sometimes be caused by infection in utero, but is often considered to have a genetic basis. Other causes of retinal detachment include inflammation, high blood pressure, advanced cases of glaucoma and uveitis, or blunt trauma.

Signs / Symptoms
Most retinal folds are discernible to the veterinary ophthalmologist from the time of the puppy's birth. In some cases, pigmentation develops as the dog ages, making the folds more difficult to detect. These malformations may cause the retina to detach from the choroid, the layer of tissue beneath the retina. The choroid is largely comprised of blood vessels. When retinal detachment occurs, the blood vessels often tear, filling the eye with blood. In addition, the detachment severs retinal cells from nerve cells that transmit visual information to the brain. Both of these factors can produce visual loss.

Retinal dysplasia is commonly diagnosed in the Akita, American Cocker Spaniel, Australian Shepherd, Beagle, Bedlington Terrier, Chow Chow, Collie, Doberman Pinscher, English Springer Spaniel, Golden Retriever, Rottweiler, Sealyham Terrier, and Yorkshire Terrier. Some breeds experience additional eye problems along with retinal dysplasia, such as colobomas: Pits or holes in the retina or choroid. In other breeds, particularly the Labrador Retriever and Samoyed, cataracts and skeletal deformities (dwarfism) are also associated with retinal dysplasia.

Prognosis

Retinal *dysplasia* is typically a non-progressive condition. In other cases of retinal detachment, the underlying cause (inflammation, glaucoma, etc.) must be addressed to minimize damage.

Treatment

Medical therapy may include antibiotics, oral diuretics, and steroids to reduce inflammation. It is also possible to "tack down" or sear the retina to the wall of the eye through laser surgery or retinopexy. This procedure can be performed in an attempt to prevent further retinal detachment. Vision restoration is not always successful, especially if the detachment is large or longstanding. At present, there are only a handful of veterinary ophthalmologists who perform retinal surgery.

As with other genetically caused eye problems, it is recommended that dogs with retinal dysplasia not be used as breeding stock. Dysplasia-prone breeds should be examined by a veterinary ophthalmologist between the ages of six and eight-and-a-half *weeks*. Examinations done later than this may not be entirely accurate.

Glaucoma

Description

Glaucoma is a condition of fluid accumulation and abnormally high pressures within the eye. This usually occurs when the trabecular meshwork (the filtration angle or drainage field) no longer functions effectively.

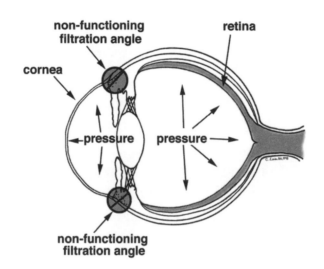

Cause

The most common cause of glaucoma in dogs results from an anatomical defect. In these cases, thin membranes of granulation tissue block the filtration angle. As the dog ages, the tissue thickens, the drainage angle narrows, and less aqueous humor is permitted to drain. This type is called primary glaucoma and typically affects both eyes.

Anatomical defects are present from birth and are considered to be genetic in nature. Commonly affected breeds include American and English Cocker Spaniel, Basset Hound, Bouvier des Flandres, Chihuahua, Dachshund, Miniature Poodle, Norwegian Elkhound, Siberian Husky, Welsh Terrier, and Wire-haired Fox Terrier. The Beagle is prone to a slightly different form of the disease.

Glaucoma can also be secondary to other problems. The drainage angle can be obstructed in a number of ways. For example, pigment fragments shed from the iris can cause blockage. Protein fragments that leak from long-standing cataracts can cause inflammation. And a tumor or dislocated lens can obstruct the angle. Such a dislocation can result from injury or a genetic predisposition. In the latter, the fibers that normally hold the lens in place weaken and rupture (lens luxation). Finally, some systemic (whole body) reactions can cause severe inflammation (uveitis), which leads to glaucoma.

Interestingly, while uveitis can *initially* cause a rise in intraocular pressure (IOP), longstanding uveitis ultimately damages the ciliary body and aqueous production, resulting in abnormally *low* IOP.

Researchers believe that several factors may contribute to blindness. Rising pressure may occlude blood vessels that nourish the retina. The cells become deprived of oxygen and natural chemicals called growth factors. Levels of glutamate — a chemical that transmits nerve and retinal cell messages — rise. High levels of glutamate allow excess calcium to enter the retinal cells, resulting in cell death. A by-product called nitric oxide accumulates and damages cells through oxidative stress (molecular damage). Retinal cells eventually die, resulting in blindness.

Signs / Symptoms
The early stages of glaucoma can present many symptoms, some of which mimic other eye problems. These can include redness, cloudiness, bulging, a dilated pupil, and loss of vision. The dog may squint or rub his eye in an attempt to relieve pain. Aggression, avoidance, and lethargy may also be reported. Extreme pain may cause shaking, panting, pacing, or vomiting in some dogs. Others may be very stoic and display few signs.

Chronic glaucoma can result in an enlarged, bulging eye. The cornea may appear blue-gray in color. As the eye stretches, additional damage can occur to internal structures.

Prognosis
Acute glaucoma is considered an emergency situation. If it is treated in time and correctly, vision can usually be maintained for some time. If the disease has gone undiagnosed or untreated, permanent blindness can result. Even with diligent treatment, it is common for the both eyes to lose vision within several years of each other. Depending on the cause of the glaucoma, the disease may affect only one eye (as with a trauma) or more often, both eyes.

Treatment

Treatment may initially include eye drops to reduce the pressure, prevent further damage, and detect whether the eye has any remaining vision. A number of eye drops may be prescribed in an attempt to reduce aqueous production. But unlike glaucoma in humans, eye drops are usually not effective in the long-term treatment of primary glaucoma in dogs. Eye drops cannot cure a structural problem.

> Note: Several medications should not be be given to dogs with glaucoma. **Atropine**, a pre-anesthesic, may raise eye pressure. **Methazolamide**, sometimes prescribed for glaucoma, alters the rate at which other medications are excreted. Consequently, methazolamide can increase *seizure activity* in epileptic dogs taking phenobarbital.

The veterinary ophthalmologist may recommend one of a several surgical procedures for your dog. He may reduce the production of aqueous fluid with cryotherapy (freezing), laser treatment, or antibiotic injection into the eye. All of these procedures scar or destroy the ciliary body (which produces aqueous). Antibiotic injection may be recommended in cases when the eye is already blind.

The doctor may recommend procedures to increase aqueous drainage. This may include implantation of a small, plastic drainage valve; surgically creating a scleral flap; or extracting a blockage, such as a dislocated lens.

If blindness is permanent and the rising pressure causes your dog pain, the veterinarian may recommend several other options. Evisceration is the removal of the internal structures of the eye (including the ciliary body) and implanting a silicone sphere. Silicone spheres are hard rubber-like balls. They are implanted behind the iris. This procedure maintains the cosmetic beauty of the dog's eye. The eye is still blind, but it looks completely normal and is no longer painful.

When a glaucomatous eye has gone untreated for longer periods, evisceration may not be a realistic option. The eye may have corneal damage or be severely inflamed. Your veterinarian may recommend enucleation (surgical removal of the eyeball and suturing the lid closed).

This can be an alarming and upsetting thought for many people. This is a normal reaction. The benefit of enucleation is that it frees the dog from constant pain. As one owner who, herself, suffers from chronic pain explains, "Relief is everything. We owe it to our dogs to keep them comfortable."

Photo of blind Beagle, "Peanut," courtesy of Lea Slaton

Following enucleation, there will be swelling and some slight discharge from the dog's nose. These dogs will retain many of their facial expressions, as the muscles will continue to function as before. These dogs possess a charm all their own, looking like the much beloved and worn stuffed toys of childhood, or as though they're winking at us.

As with other genetically caused eye problems, it is recommended that dogs with primary glaucoma not be used for breeding.

Cataracts

Description
Cataracts are sometimes mistakenly described as a film over the eye. This is not an accurate description. Dogs that develop cataracts experience a change in the protein found in the lens. The normally clear lens turns progressively opaque. The opacity prevents light from reaching the retina. This white, opaque lens is the cataract.

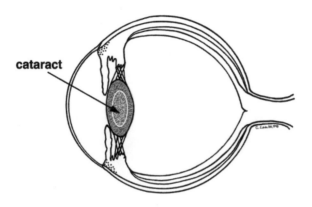

Cause
The most common cause of canine cataracts differs from the most common cause in humans. Most humans will develop cataracts as a normal part of aging. Cataract development in dogs often occurs at a comparatively younger age — between four months to three years. These cataracts are usually caused by a genetic predisposition. Affected breeds include Afghan Hound, American and English Cocker Spaniel, Australian Terrier, Boston Terrier, Chesapeake Bay Retriever, German Shepherd Dog, Golden Retriever, Labrador Retriever, Miniature and Standard Poodle, Miniature Schnauzer, Old English Sheepdog, Rottweiler, Staffordshire Bull Terrier, Welsh Springer Spaniel, and West Highland White Terrier.

There are several other causes of cataracts. Diabetes mellitus results in high levels of glucose (sugar) circulating in the bloodstream. Researchers believe that this sugar accumulates in the lens and causes irreversible damage to the lens fibers. Most diabetic dogs will eventually develop cataracts within twelve to eighteen months of diagnosis. However, the better the glucose control, the greater the chance of forestalling cataract development and other complications. (See page 184 for diabtetic-dog resources.)

Cushing's disease can also contribute to cataracts. It is unclear whether the contributing factor is the high level of circulating steroids, glucose, or both.

Cataracts can also be caused by trauma or injury to the eye. The lens appears to shatter. Puppies can be born with congenital cataracts or develop them when fed milk-replacement formula deficient in necessary amino acids.

Finally, there are also some instances of normal, age-related changes in the lens that are different than the genetically caused cataracts diagnosed in younger dogs. This condition is termed nuclear sclerosis, which does not typically result in significant vision loss.

Signs / Symptoms
Initially, a white glare from the dog's eyes may be noticeable in certain lighting. Eventually, the glare will be visible all the time. The iris may become increasingly dilated, as the body attempts to supply more light to the retina. At this stage, dogs may have difficulty functioning in the glare of bright lights.

Finally, the lens will be completely opaque, causing total blindness. Behavioral changes may include a hesitancy to jump, failure to judge distance, and bumping into objects.

Prognosis
Hereditary cataracts typically progress slowly — from six months to several years. They will progress to complete blindness if left untreated. Hereditary cataracts typically do not cause an animal discomfort.

Cataracts resulting from diabetes and Cushing's disease can progress to blindness within mere days or weeks. In cases of long-standing cataracts, the lens capsule may crack. This allows protein fragments to shed into the aqueous fluid. These fragments may block the filtration angle and cause glaucoma. They may also inflame the eye, causing uveitis. Glaucoma and uveitis can cause the dog severe discomfort.

The veterinary ophthalmologist can make a more accurate prognosis by performing an ERG or electroretinogram on your dog. This test is valuable since retinal degeneration sometimes accompanies cataract formation.

Treatment

If there are no complicating factors present, surgical removal of cataracts is most often the recommended treatment. Many veterinary ophthalmologists perform this procedure in the same manner it's performed on humans.

If cataract surgery is recommended and financially feasible, the prognosis is usually quite good. While it is difficult to put a statistical figure on the success rate of surgery, the outcome is usually improved vision. It is important to remember that each dog is an individual and will heal differently. Surgical risks do include glaucoma, retinal detachment, and uveitis.

The surgeon makes an incision near the edge of the cornea and most often inserts the tip of a small instrument called a phaco-emulsifier. It pulverizes the lens with ultrasound waves and then flushes away the fragments. Frequently, the surgeon implants a plastic implant lens or intraocular lens (IOL). Follow-up exams are an important part of a successful recovery.

There are a few instances when surgery is not recommended. The first instance is in the case of long-standing or hypermature cataracts. In these cases, the protein in the lens may have liquefied and leaked into the eye. Such an eye may be severely inflamed. These eyes are not good surgical candidates. Instead, the ophthalmologist may prescribe anti-inflammatory eye drops.

Additionally, surgery is not recommended if the ERG demonstrates poor retinal function. It would be useless to remove the cataracts and allow light into the eye if the retina is unable to process those light waves.

Dogs with hereditary cataracts should not be used as breeding stock. In addition, the parents or siblings or these dogs should not be used for breeding. If any puppy in the litter is afflicted, it means some of the other puppies will be carriers. Without knowing which dog is a carrier and which dog is unaffected, breeding any of the dogs from this type of litter can reproduce the disease.

Congenital Malformations

Micro-ophthalmia means that a puppy is born with incompletely developed, small eyes. These dogs may have low vision, or may be completely blind depending on the degree of development. Anophthalmia means that the eyes do not develop at all. One common cause of congenital malformations is a hereditary condition known as Collie Eye Anomaly.

Parasites, Bacterial, Viral, and Other Infections

A number of infectious or parasitic infestations can cause blindness. The distemper virus can cause retinal inflammation (retinitis) or detachment. Such damage can follow an actual distemper infection or modified-live distemper vaccine. Blastomycosis, ehrlichiosis, leptospirosis, and toxoplasmosis can result in glaucoma, uveitis, or retinal detachment.

Uveodermatologic Syndrome (UDS)
or Vogt-Koyanagi-Harada Syndrome (VKH)

This syndrome involves an autoimmune attack on the pigmented cells of the skin and retina. In autoimmune diseases, antibodies that have been previously programmed to attack a foreign amino acid chain (such as a virus or dietary protein) mistakenly attack the pigmented layers of the retina. A number of owners report the onset of UDS to follow the dog's annual vaccines. Many also report that their dogs experience concurrent autoimmune thyroid disease.

Ophthalmic aspects of this syndrome include retinal inflammation, glaucoma, retinal detachment, and blindness. It can be a painful condition for the dog. Early treatment is most beneficial.

Treatment involves high doses of steroids and other immune system depressants in order to minimize the autoimmune attack. Since the immune system will be severely depressed, many veterinarians will advise against vaccines for these dogs. Prognosis for canine UDS patients is variable. The effects of the steroid treatment (hunger, thirst, incontinence, confusion, lethargy, etc.) can diminish quality of life in their own way.

Trauma

Blunt injury can result in proptosis (bulging) or complete displacement of the eye. Anatomy can play a role in such problems. Breeding dogs for short muzzles results in more shallow eye sockets. These eyes are more prone to injury and may be inevitably lost, even with good emergency treatment.

Blindness Due to Transient Ischemia in Epilepsy

Seizures that occur in the occipital lobe of the brain have long been associated with transient, bilateral blindness. This is referred to as cortical blindness. It is unclear as to whether the blindness results from hypoxia (oxygen deprivation) of the brain cells or if the seizure disrupts visual recognition in some other way. Temporary blindness may last a few hours or days. In some cases, damage is more permanent.

Canine Senility

It is important to make one point that can confuse issues of blindness. There are indeed cases of canine senility. Symptoms of senility can include a dog walking into a corner and being unable to find his way back out, staring into space, and incessant barking. It is important to seek veterinary help to diagnose and treat your dog's vision loss. Treatment can include such drugs as Anipryl or the nutritional supplement Phosphatidyl Serine. These help reduce the production of the stress hormone, cortisol, which is known for its damaging effects on the short-term memory and cognitive function.

References

American College of Veterinary Ophthalmologists, *Ocular Disorders Presumed to be Inherited in Dogs*. West Lafayette: Canine Eye Registration Foundation, 1996.

Blaylock, R.L., *Excitotoxins: The Taste That Kills*. Santa Fe: Health Press, 1994.

Brooks, D.E., Garcia, G.A., Dreyer, E.B., et al, "Vitreous Body Glutamate Concentrations in Dogs with Glaucoma," *American Journal of Veterinary Research*, 58: 1997.

Carmody, R.J., and Cotter, T.G., "Oxidative Stress Induces Caspase-independent Retinal Apoptosis in Vitro," *Cell Death Differentiation*, 7(3): March, 2000.

Councell, C., et al, "Coexistence of Celiac and Thyroid Disease," *Gut*, 35(6): June, 1994.

Cutolo, M., and Wilder, R., "Different Roles for Androgens and Estrogens in the Susceptibility to Autoimmune Rheumatic Diseases," *Rheumatic Diseases Clinics of North America*, 26: 2000.

Gulcan, H.G., Alvarez, R.A., Maude, M.B., Adnerson, R.E., "Lipids of Human Retina, Retinal Pigment Epithelium, and Bruch's Membrane/Choroid: Comparison of Macular and Peripheral Regions," *Investigative Ophthalmology and Visual Science*, 34(11): October, 1993.

Horger, B.A., and Roth, R.H., "Stress and Central Amino Acid System," *Neurobiological and Clinical Consequences of Stress: From Adaptation to PTSD*. Lippincott-Raven: Philadelphia, 1995.

Kidd, Parris M., *Phosphatidylserine: The Nutrient Building Block That Accelerates All Brain Functions and Counters Alzheimer's*. New Cannan, Conn.: Keats Publishing, Inc., 1998.

Lechin, F., van der Dijs, B., Lechin, A.E., Orozco, B., Lechin, M.E., Baez, S., et al, "Plasma Neurotransmitters and Cortisol in Chronic Illness: Role of Stress." *Journal of Medicine*, 25: 1994.

Levin, C.D., *Dogs, Diet and Disease: An Owner's Guide to Diabetes Mellitus, Pancreatitis, Cushing's Disease, and More*. Oregon City: Lantern Publications, 2001.

McLellan, G.J., Elks, R., Lybaert, P., Watté, C., Moore, D., and Bedford, P. G.C., "Vitamin E Deficiency in Canine Retinal Pigment Epithelial Dystrophy," *Veterinary Record*, 151: 2002.

Nickells, R.W., "Retinal Ganglion Cell Death in Glaucoma: The How, the Why and the Maybe," *Journal of Glaucoma*, 123(6): 1996.

Nieman, L.K., "Diagnostic Tests for Cushing's Syndrome," *Annals of the New York Academy of Sciences*, 970: September, 2002.

Nockels, C.F., Odde, K.G., and Craig, A.M., "Vitamin E. Supplementation and Stress Affect Tissue Alpha-tocopherol Content of Beef Heifers," *Journal of Animal Science*, 74(3): 1996.

Plechner, A., Zucker, M., *Pets at Risk: From Allergies to Cancer, Remedies for an Unsuspected Epidemic*, Troutdale, Oregon: New Sage Press, 2003.

Raber, J., "Detrimental Effects of Chronic Hypothalamic-Pituitary-Adrenal Axis Activation," *Molecular Neurobiology*, August, 1998.

Rosenberger, B., *Life Itself: Exploring the Realm of the Living Cell*. Oxford: Oxford Press, 1998.

Sapolsky, R.M., *Why Zebras Don't Get Ulcers: An Updated Guide to Stress, Stress Related Disease, and Coping*. New York: W.H. Freeman & Co., 1998.

Sarjeant, D., and Evans, K., *Hard to Swallow: The Truth About Food Additives*. Burnaby, BC: Alive Books, 1999.

Slatter, D., *Fundamentals of Veterinary Ophthalmology*. Philadelphia: W.B. Saunders Company, 2001.

GENETICS AND BLINDNESS

The study of genetics is a complex and ever-evolving science. This basic overview will help dog owners understand how some forms of blindness are passed down from parents to offspring. If you are not a breeder, it is important for you to notify the breeder of your dog regarding his blindness. Good breeders will take this information into account as they consider future matings. They do not want to encourage diseases in the breeds they love.

Some blinding conditions are generally defined as dominant genetic disorders. Others are defined as recessive genetic disorders. The latter includes many cases (but not all) of PRA and hereditary cataracts. In many conditions, the mode of inheritance is not clearly defined. These disorders may involve multiple pairs of genes or may involve a combination of genetic and environmental factors.

If you are a breeder and are interested in the mode of inheritance in your particular breed, consult your veterinary ophthalmologist or the text *Ocular Disorders Presumed to be Inherited in Dogs* written by the Genetics Committee of the American College of Veterinary Ophthalmologists. (See *Suppliers* section.)

Genetic Laws

In most cases of heritable blindness, the dog has two genes for this disease. The dog inherits one of these genes from his mother and the other gene from his father. Based on how they express themselves (behave), genes are generally defined as either dominant or recessive.

When one dominant gene is paired together with one recessive gene, the dominant gene will *win out*, so to speak. In other words, it will dictate the biological outcome of the dog. Scientists refer to a gene that is dominant by using a capital letter, such as "A."

When no dominant genes are present, recessive genes have a chance to dictate the biological outcome. Scientists refer to a recessive gene by a lower case letter, such as "a." Some forms of blindness are carried on a dominant gene, while others are carried on a recessive gene.

The Law of Simple Dominance —
Disorders Carried on a Recessive Gene

As previously mentioned, two of the most common blinding diseases are caused by genetic faults. They are generalized PRA and cataracts. In *most* cases, these diseases are defined as recessive genetic disorders, because the disease is carried on the recessive or "a" gene.

There are three possible types of gene pairs in recessive genetic disorders:

- Some dogs inherit a normal, dominant gene from each parent. These dogs are denoted as "AA." Since these dogs have two dominant genes, the healthy ones, these dogs will appear normal and *are* normal. They have no faulty genes to pass along to offspring.

- Other dogs inherit one normal, dominant gene from one parent ("A") and one faulty, recessive gene from the other ("a"). Since the normal gene is the dominant one, these dogs will appear normal (exhibit no outward signs of the disease), but they will always carry around one faulty gene. These dogs may pass on this faulty gene to their offspring. They are called carriers and are denoted as "Aa." If a carrier is used for breeding, there is a fifty percent chance that the dog will pass along the faulty gene to puppies. Mathematically, this plays a significant role in the proliferation of PRA and cataracts.

- Finally, some dogs inherit a recessive gene from each parent. These dogs are denoted as "aa." Since the disease is carried on recessive genes and these dogs have two affected genes, they will be affected by the disease. If bred, these dogs will always contribute one faulty gene to their puppies.

The following are the possible outcomes in reference to simple recessive genetic disorders.

- Breeding a normal dog to a normal dog ("AA" x "AA"):
    All of the puppies would be normal ("AA")

- Breeding a normal dog to a carrier dog ("AA" x "Aa"):
    50% of the puppies would be normal ("AA")
    50% of the puppies would be carriers ("Aa")

- Breeding a normal dog to an afflicted dog ("AA" x "aa"):
    All of the puppies would be carriers ("Aa")

- Breeding a carrier to a carrier ("Aa" x "Aa"):
    25% of the puppies would be normal ("AA")
    50% of the puppies would be carriers ("Aa")
    25% of the puppies would be afflicted ("aa")

- Breeding a carrier to an afflicted dog ("Aa" x "aa"):
    50% of the puppies would be carriers ("Aa")
    50% of the puppies would be afflicted ("aa")

- Breeding an afflicted dog to an afflicted dog ("aa" x "aa"):
    All of the puppies would be afflicted

It is tempting to believe that since breeding an afflicted dog to a normal mate would only result in carriers, this would be a reasonable thing to do. Unfortunately, in many cases, it's impossible to distinguish a carrier from a healthy dog since neither demonstrates any symptoms of the disease. Therefore, odds are good that by breeding any afflicted dog, these blinding diseases will be proliferated. It is also recommended against breeding the littermates of the afflicted dog, since we know that about half of them will be carriers. A repeat breeding of the parents is not recommended either. They will reproduce more afflicted and carrier puppies.

The Law of Incomplete Dominance
Disorders Carried on a Dominant Gene

In these instances, the gene that carries the disease is a dominant gene. Collie eye anomaly and merle-colored coats follow this pattern. Cataracts found in the Beagle, Chesapeake Bay Retriever, German Shepherd Dog, and Labrador Retriever are suspected to follow this pattern. PRA in the Bullmastiff and English Mastiff does, too. In these cases we see three *other* possible gene pairs:

The three types of possible gene pairs in dominant genetic disorders:

- Some dogs inherit a normal, in this case, recessive gene from each parent. These dogs are denoted as "aa." Since these dogs have two healthy genes, these dogs will appear normal and *are* normal. They have no faulty genes to pass along to offspring.

- Other dogs inherit a normal, recessive gene from one parent ("a") and a faulty but dominant gene from the other ("A"). Since the faulty gene is a dominant one, it will *win out* over the recessive gene and these dogs will be partially affected with the disease. These dogs *may* pass on the faulty gene to any offspring and are denoted as "Aa."

- Finally, there are dogs that inherit a dominant and, in this case, defective gene from each parent. They are denoted as "AA" and are fully affected by the disease. If bred, these dogs will *always* contribute one faulty, dominant gene to their puppies.

The following are the possible outcomes in reference to incomplete dominant genetic disorders.

- Breeding a normal dog to a normal dog ("aa" x "aa"):
    All of the puppies would be normal ("aa")

- Breeding a normal dog to a partially affected dog ("aa" x "Aa"):
    50% of the puppies would be normal ("aa")
    50% of the puppies would be partially affected ("Aa")

- Breeding a normal dog to a fully affected dog ("aa" x "AA"):
    All of the puppies would be partially affected ("Aa")

- Breeding a partially affected dog to a partially affected dog ("Aa" x "Aa"):
    25% of the puppies would be normal ("aa")
    50% of the puppies would be partially affected ("Aa")
    25% of the puppies would be fully affected ("AA")

- Breeding a partially affected dog to a fully affected dog ("Aa" x "AA"):
    50% of the puppies would be partially affected ("Aa")
    50% of the puppies would be fully affected ("AA")

- Breeding two fully affected dogs ("AA" x "AA"):
    All of the puppies would be fully affected

On a positive note, researchers continue to develop genetic testing methods. Such tests may help breeders identify carriers from normal canines. This may slowly help reduce the incidence of genetically caused blindness. Please consult your veterinary ophthalmologist or the Optigen Corporation (see *Suppliers* section) for details and availability of genetic testing.

It is sometimes difficult for geneticists to determine the mode of transmission for any particular condition. A good example of this is retinal dysplasia. In many cases, retinal dysplasia is defined as a recessive disorder. When it is coupled with dwarfism, however, it is defined as a dominant disorder. Another confusing issue is that the mode of inheritance for the same condition may differ between breeds.

This may cause confusion for dog breeders wanting to know which animals are safe to breed. It is not recommended to breed any blind dogs. The American College of Veterinary Ophthalmologists recommends against breeding individuals with the following disorders:

- Cataracts — unless cleared by the veterinary ophthalmologist

- Lens luxation or subluxation — the lens becomes dislocated or loose

- Glaucoma

- Persistent hyperplastic primary vitreous — a developmental defect in which the hyaloid artery fails to regress, leaving the lens connected to the vitreous

- Retinal detachment

- Retinal dysplasia

- Optic nerve coloboma — a developmental defect in which the sclera is pitted and the optic nerve may be damaged

- Progressive Retinal Atrophy

In summary, responsible breeders strive to produce healthy puppies. They screen or test their breeding stock. And, they alter their breeding program in an attempt not to reproduce faulty genes. It is a difficult and often uncertain process.

Interestingly, genetic predisposition (the genetic code) is probably not the sole culprit in these diseases. Advances in healthcare implicate environmental factors as triggers for genetic predispositions. In other words, genetic conditions are likely a combination of both genetic code and an environmental stressor. For a more detailed discussion of this topic, please see Chapter 16, *Vision and the Modern-Day Dog*.

References

American College of Veterinary Ophthalmologists, *Ocular Disorders Presumed to be Inherited in Dogs*. West Lafayette: Canine Eye Registration Foundation, 1996.

Optigen staff, "Testing for (Old English) Mastiff and Bullmastiff Dominant PRA," *http://www.optigen.com*, April 28, 2003.

Rosenberger, B., *Life Itself: Exploring the Realm of the Living Cell*. Oxford: Oxford Press, 1998.

HOW DOGS REACT TO BLINDNESS

Think of the dogs you have known over the years. Like people, dogs are individuals. And because they are individuals, dogs react to blindness differently. Some become depressed or aggressive. Some become dependant. Others exhibit no behavioral changes whatsoever. The following factors contribute to how well a dog adapts to blindness.

- **The dog's age** — is he young and enthusiastic or is he making this adjustment after spending most of his life as a sighted dog?

- **His general health** — is he fit and capable of learning new skills or does he have health problems that will be compounded by blindness?

- **The onset of blindness** — was it sudden, as with SARD, or was the dog able to compensate gradually?

- **Previous training experiences** — is your dog used to having you work with him or is he a fringe member of the family?

- **His personality and position in the pack** — is he a confident, dominant dog; a worried, submissive dog; or somewhere in between?

- **The age, health, and personalities of other dogs in the household** — will they help the blind dog or compete for his pack position?

- **Your dedication and interest** — do you have the time and desire to train and encourage your dog?

In general, dogs that go blind gradually, early in life, and are not pack leaders, make a faster and easier adjustment to blindness. Older, frail, dominant dogs, and those that lose their vision suddenly, can sometimes experience more difficulty. Blind-dog owners report that this adjustment can typically take three to six months. But certainly there are instances where it has taken longer to adjust. It is possible for you to help ease this transition in a number of ways.

The Fight-or-Flight Response

Since a dog cannot understand what is happening and since we cannot communicate that to him, we can only surmise what is going through the dog's mind. One animal behaviorist believes that animals perceive physical ailments akin to being attacked by another animal. There are similarities between the responses of a sick (or blind) dog and a dog being attacked, so there may be some value in this concept.

Dogs have a strong fight-or-flight response. Based on a variety of factors, a dog may stand up and fight challenges (attackers) or he may flee (run from attackers). Neither response is wrong. They are both effective survival mechanisms and don't have any reflection on a dog's intelligence or virtue.

Fear and Aggression

If, indeed, a dog responds to blindness as though it is an attacker, he may try to fight. If your dog was dominant and aggressive before the blindness, this may become more apparent now. Similarly, if your dog was a fearful individual before the blindness, this may now manifest itself as aggression because fear and aggression are closely linked.

Without the ability to identify a true attacker, the dog may lash out. He may snarl, snap, and bite other pack members, family, and friends. This is a common reaction.

There is a fine line to handling these situations successfully. On one hand, aggression is not behavior that you should encourage or accept. On the other hand, the dog is already stressed and fearful. A strong reprimand could serve to escalate the situation into a full-fledged attack.

Try to minimize whatever situations incite the aggression — other dogs sniffing him, visitors, etc. Issue a calm reprimand. Do not pet, cuddle, or otherwise reward the dog after the aggressive behavior. That will only encourage the dog to repeat it. As you progress with training, specific activities will be outlined to help you deal with this issue.

Depression

Dogs that try to fight the blindness obviously don't succeed. And for some dogs, fighting isn't their first instinct. These dogs would typically flee an aggressor. Unfortunately for these dogs, fleeing is not a realistic option either. The blindness follows them everywhere. Ultimately, for many dogs, their normal methods of coping are ineffective.

Dog trainers know that show-ring dogs can have a similar experience. Many dogs become stressed in the show-ring because there is no specific aggressor to fight and they are unable to flee the environment. These dogs become overwhelmed. They begin moving slowly. They lower their heads, ears, and tails. In effect, they become depressed.

Depression is a common and normal reaction to blindness. A few dogs have difficulty getting past this state. Dogs can demonstrate a decrease in activity (play) and an increase in daytime sleeping. They have less interest in toys or tasks that once brought them pleasure. One owner reported his dog standing in the center of the room and simply crying.

Photo of blind dog, "Polly," courtesy of Joyce Carothers

In cases of SARD, depression may have an actual physical cause. Excess production of cortisol (the stress hormone) reduces levels of normal, beneficial brain chemicals. Initiating methods to reduce cortisol production may help your dog better adjust to blindness.

If you are experiencing depression over your dog's blindness, it is possible that you are transmitting these feelings to your dog, as well. Most dogs take their emotional cues from their owners. While it is important for dog owners to grieve, it may be beneficial to shield the dog from these emotions. Separate yourself from the dog when you feel especially sad or need to cry. Give the dog a chew toy and move into another room. You will have to evaluate the fine line between shielding your dog and any separation anxiety he might have.

Another method of dealing with depression is through massage. You need not be an expert at this skill for your dog to benefit. Unless he experiences other physical discomfort, general massage over the dog's neck and back can be an enjoyable experience for both of you.

Massage can be performed daily, if you have the time. But even massage done just twice weekly is effective in lowering cortisol levels in humans. Make certain that you are in a peaceful state of mind before you begin. Breath slowly, deeply, and evenly.

Start by stroking from the bridge of his nose and over the top of his head. Work down his neck, back, and toward his tail. As you massage, pay attention to your dog's reaction. If he slinks down, avoids the motion, or rolls over to hide an area of his body, it may be a sign of discomfort. Avoid such areas. Finish off the massage by gently rubbing his ears.

It is believed that massage can both calm a stressed dog and energize a lethargic dog. It is also a way to reconnect with your dog since he can no longer see you. Tactile (touch) stimulation is a good way to keep him connected to his environment.

Dependency

Some dogs exhibit an increased tendency toward dependency. These dogs become increasingly hesitant to perform tasks for themselves. They may barely be willing to walk across a room, let alone attempt a flight of stairs. In these situations, the owner finds himself doing more and more for the dog. Both blind and sighted dogs can become masters at manipulating their people.

Dependency is an attitude, which unknowingly, can be rewarded by the owner. For many of us, pets awaken our maternal, caring instincts. It's normal to want to help them. While it is important to recognize handicaps the blind dog might have, it is equally important not to coddle him. Coddling is the enemy to any progress your dog might make. This is a sentiment repeated over and over by blind-dog owners. Do not allow your dog to become dependent upon you. Once coddling stops and training begins, your dog can regain confidence in himself and the world around him.

"Leo," a blind Shih-Tzu

References

Field, T., "Massage Therapy," Medical Clinics of North America, 86(1): January, 2002.

PACK ISSUES
AND BEHAVIORIAL CHANGES

If you were planning a trip to a foreign country, you would likely take time to study the culture and language. This would be beneficial since cultures communicate differently. In some cultures, we greet each other by shaking hands. In other cultures, we kiss cheeks. And, in yet others, we bow.

Dogs say, "hello," quite differently than do we. It is important to realize that dogs, too, have a culture all their own. It is valuable to understand their language as we try to communicate with them. This knowledge will also help us understand how blindness affects dogs.

The typical canine greeting.

Pack Structure

The normal canine social structure is the pack. Many people do not realize the all-encompassing importance pack life has for a dog. The organization of the pack governs most canine behaviors and communications.

Wolves have existed in packs for thousands of years. Typically, there is a male leader called an alpha (first) dog. There is also an alpha female. The remainder of the pack is structured in a descending hierarchy: A beta male and female, a gamma male and female, and so on.

Domesticated dogs may have several different species in their packs including humans and, in some instances, cats or farm animals. Domesticated dogs typically have a leader amongst the dogs, as well as a human leader over the entire pack. It is best if all humans, including children, are viewed as more dominant members of the pack.

Ranking in the Pack — Dominance and Submission

In human society, we like to think of all men as being created equal. In the dog pack this is not so. Difficult as it may be, we need to accept this. The pack is structured in such a way as to promote cooperation and ensure the survival of its members. If all dogs or wolves were equals, there would be no distinct leader to protect the pack from danger.

A dog's position in the pack is decided by several factors: Age, his basic personality, and how the other pack members react to him. Dogs that rank higher in the pack (are more dominant) are entitled to more privileges. They get the best sleeping places and expect other pack members to move aside as they pass. Dominant dogs defend their food by growling and may steal food or toys from other dogs. They mount or stand over these dogs. They mark their territory with urine.

Submissive dogs range from beta (a happy-go-lucky individual that might take control if circumstances dictated) to omega (a sometimes fearful, anxious dog). Submissive dogs yield to more dominant pack members. They relinquish toys, food, and their sleeping spots.

Submission is not synonymous with cowardice or punishment. In the dog's culture, it is a form of cooperation. It is important for us to realize that dogs are content with this arrangement. They typically don't mind being in any particular position in the pack. They just want to know where their position is.

Blind Dogs and Body Language

Dogs declare their pack position with body language. Since blind dogs can no longer read body language, this can be problematic. It can be especially challenging when dogs meet for the first time. It can be helpful for *you* to understand what body language indicates during introductions.

Dominant (and sometimes aggressive) dogs display signs such as lunging forward, standing upright, raised hair on their neck, and a stiff, upright tail. Dominant dogs stare at more submissive dogs.

Playful, sub-alpha dogs may exhibit behaviors much like dominant dogs. A few important differences include bouncing, dancing, or play bowing and an open, laughing mouth.

Submissive dogs display the following signs: They roll over, allow other dogs to sniff them, avert their gaze, and make themselves appear smaller by getting closer to the ground.

Fearful (and sometimes aggressive) dogs may demonstrate behaviors similar to submissive dogs. They carry their ears, head, and tail down or tucked. However, the fearful dog will not allow his underside to be sniffed. He may raise his hackle and growl. These are *warning signs*. Do not dismiss them. The dog that displays these behaviors may handle his fear by biting, hence the term *fear biter*. Some fear biters give *no* warning.

Humans as Pack Leaders

In order to gain cooperation from dogs, they must view you as the ultimate pack leader. Humans must communicate to the dogs in ways they will understand. That is, similar to alpha dogs. This does not necessarily mean that an owner must growl at his dog.

Many people do not effectively communicate their leadership position to their dogs. These owners may give verbal commands and then fail to enforce them. They retreat if the dog growls at them. They may routinely put the dog's wishes before their own.

As humans, we want others to like us. We may feel uncomfortable enforcing rules to our beloved pets. Dogs don't view things this way. Their comfort and peace of mind comes from an orderly and structured social setting. We do our dogs a kindness when we communicate as a reliable, consistent pack leader.

If we demonstrate submissive behaviors that are inconsistent with the alpha position, we confuse the dog. If a dog concludes that there is no real pack-leader, his instinct will be to rise to that position himself. This instinct would insure the continued survival of the wild pack.

This instinct also represents the core of many behavioral problems we see in domesticated dogs today. When a dog does not regard his human pack members to be higher ranking, the dog may challenge them in an attempt to take control himself. This is normal behavior on the dog's part. This does not represent a nasty or poorly bred dog. It represents a language-barrier between two cultures. For a human to be a leader it does not require rough treatment, just consistency.

Separation From the Pack

In the wild, there is safety in remaining close to other pack members. If a single wolf is separated from the pack, he becomes vulnerable to attack by other animals. This may explain a little bit about the separation anxiety that so many dogs experience when their owners leave the house without them.

With blindness comes a visual separation from you, the dog's leader. It is alarming for some dogs to be unable to find the other members of their pack. Some owners report that their dog has less tolerance to being crated or kenneled after the onset of blindness.

In living with a blind dog you will be able to capitalize on his amazing senses of hearing and smell. However, it is important to remember that blindness may cause some dogs a sense of separation and insecurity. This will be an important concept to remember when you take your dog out in public.

When Dominant Dogs Go Blind

Another aspect of blindness involves the concept of survival-of-the-fittest. This concept specifically applies to dominant dogs. Since a blind dog is unable to read the body language of other dogs, he may not respond with the same alpha behaviors he once did. Consequently, other dogs may challenge his position of leadership — even attack him.

Some behaviorists recommend letting dogs determine their pack order by themselves. Other experts believe that, as the true pack leaders, humans should forbid any type of fighting or aggression. If the blind dog has always been an alpha dog, it may be beneficial to help him retain this position.

Such efforts on your part may reduce pack tensions and aggression in your house. If the blind dog is also elderly or immuno-compromised, it is important to minimize injuries since the healing process will be delayed in these animals.

Assisting the Dominant Blind Dog

It is your job, as the true pack leader, to enforce good manners in your pack. Be alert during mealtime. If others try to steal the blind dog's food, physically separate the dogs. You may also separate the feedings by a few minutes so the blind dog can eat first. Sometimes a combination of both is necessary.

In the wild, dominant wolves eat first from the prey they have killed. You can promote the blind dogs dominant position by feeding him dinner before the other dogs. For serious cases, you can feed him a special treat or biscuit in front of, but not including, the other dogs.

Since dominant dogs typically pass through doorways before subordinate dogs, help your blind dog through the door first. This may require physically restraining the other dogs, while verbally encouraging the blind one. If this proves too difficult, allow the blind dog outdoors separately from the others.

When you are expecting company, restrain all of the pack except the blind dog. A baby gate across the door of an adjoining room works nicely. Allow the blind dog to greet your guests first. If necessary, help the blind dog find the visitors.

Make sure the blind alpha dog has a special, more privileged bed or sleeping place. Since people all live differently with their dogs, special can take on different meanings. Regardless of where your dogs sleep at night, the closer the sleeping spot is to you, the more privileged a position it is.

If your dogs sleep outdoors, an indoor sleeping spot would be a privileged position. If the dogs sleep indoors, the bedroom would be the privilege spot. If all your dogs sleep on the bed with you, it might be the spot closest to you.

Verbal reprimands are appropriate to enforce the manners of your dogs. Be conscious of how the blind dog reacts to your raised voice, though. He might think the reprimand is directed at him! A silent method of correcting other pack members is to use a spray-bottle filled with water.

When Sub-alpha Dogs Go Blind

Few dogs are truly alpha. Dogs that are more subordinate may not require the type of intervention mentioned above. These dogs share the leadership role and can generally be described as sub-alpha. Sub-alpha dogs seem less threatened by blindness. These dogs frequently follow the cues of sighted pack members. Owners with two sub-alpha dogs report that the second one acts as a seeing-eye dog for the blind animal.

Photo of Labrador Retrievers, "Pilot" chaperoning "Maggie" (blind), courtesy of Catherine Jamieson

Adding a Sighted Dog to Your Pack

If your blind dog is a sub-alpha and is the only dog in the household, consider acquiring a second, sub-alpha dog as a companion. (If the blind dog is extremely dominant, he may not accept the help of a second dog. And, if the new addition is extremely dominant, he may not be interested in helping the blind dog.)

Owners report numerous instances in which their sub-alpha dogs assist the blind one. The sighted dog may bark in order to help the blind dog locate him. In other cases, the blind dog may bark for his sighted companion to escort him from the yard to the house.

If possible, allow the dogs to meet on neutral territory in order to assess their compatibility. Neutral territory can include a park or the fenced yard of an animal shelter. Some dogs find introductions off leash less threatening.

Allow the blind dog several months to adjust to his condition before adding a second dog. Sometimes, but certainly not always, a male and female dog will be more compatible than two males or two females. If your blind dog is quite elderly, consider adding a dog that is past puppyhood. Puppies can pester older dogs and due to their young age it may be some time before they begin to help the blind dog.

Adding a Blind Dog Into Your Sighted Pack

Adopting or fostering a blind dog is an admirable act. People involved in such rescue work offer the following advice.

Prepare your house before you leave to pick up the new dog. Confine your pack to one part of the house. Bring in the new dog, on leash, and allow him to investigate the other part of the house. He will be able to smell your other dogs' scents. Then put him in a crate. Place a wire exercise pen (ex-pen) around the crate for added security.

Next, allow the members of your pack, only one at a time, into the area to sniff and see the new arrival. Begin with the most dominant dog. After an hour or so, unlatch the door of the crate. The new comer will push open the door when he is ready. Stay close.

If any of your pack shows aggression by growling or posturing, correct that behavior with the water bottle. Reward quiet behavior verbally or with a food treat. If you identify aggressive behavior it will be best to maintain the ex-pen arrangement for some time. This may mean several weeks.

In the meantime, build a relationship with the new dog. This will be accomplished during private grooming, play, and training sessions. This one-on-one contact will help the new dog bond with you as the true pack leader. (For additional guidance on pack leadership, see page 168, Dawn Jecs' *Simply Living*.)

Assess the personality of the blind dog before you introduce him to new dogs. There are three probable scenarios when dogs meet for the first time:

• The new dog likes most dogs and would enjoy meeting other dogs.

• The new dog is somewhat dominant *or* insecure, may feel threatened, and possibly attack or be attacked by the other dogs.

• The new dog is somewhat submissive and insecure and may be frightened by meeting other dogs.

Making a Safe Spot

Regardless of pack position, it is recommended that all blind dogs have a special place to which they can retreat. This is valuable when the commotion of daily life becomes too much for them. A safe spot provides the blind dog with a resting place where he does not have to worry about who is going to sneak up on him. A safe spot is frequently an area other than his nighttime sleeping spot.

Wolves and dogs are den animals. They retreat to a small, protected area for safety. An ideal retreat for your dog would be a dog bed, dog crate, or kennel. A safe spot can even be a particular chair or corner of the couch.

If you are using a crate or kennel, leave the door open so he may come and go as he pleases. The exception would be if you use the crate to keep the dog safe and contained while you are unable to supervise or are out of the house.

Place the bed or crate in an area where the family spends most of its time, but avoid high-traffic paths. In this way, the blind dog can safely retreat from activity, but maintain social contact. Experiment with different spots.

It is possible that other dogs in your household will seek out the blind dog's bed. In this case, beds may be in order for everyone! The key is to enforce the blind dog's ability to have a place he can always call his own. You may need to verbally correct other dogs that try to take his spot or physically remove them.

As dogs age, it may become necessary to change the location of a dog's safe spot or to improve access. Some owners move the pet's bed from the couch to the floor. This prevents jumping injuries and accidental falls. Other owners implement ramps to help small dogs climb onto couches and beds. One owner recommends a sleeping wedge, a foam pillow designed to elevate one's head. Placed along the front of the couch, it provides easy access for the dog. (See *Suppliers* section for ramps.)

Identification of Other Pack Members

Sound plays a large part in the blind dog's ability to identify and locate other pack members. Some blind dogs become fearful and aggressive when surprised by the arrival of another pack member.

Purchase a variety of small bells for the collars of the other dogs in the household. Blind dogs can use this sound as a beacon. It will help them follow and find the sighted dogs. It's possible, with a little effort, to find bells of different sizes and styles. This variation of sounds may assist the blind dog in associating a particular sound with a particular pack member.

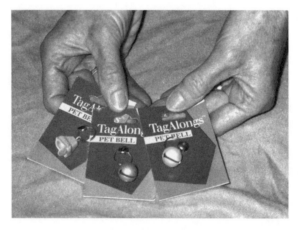

Consider putting a bell on yourself or in your pocket. This can help the blind dog find you, his leader, around the house and yard. It can also be of help if your dog is uncomfortable in the crate. Wearing a bell will help reassure the dog that you are near. A wide variety of fashion accessories are usually available around Christmastime. Dress shops and department stores carry jewelry, scarves, socks, etc. with bells attached.

If you'd prefer not to wear a bell and your dog continues to be surprised by your arrival, announce yourself as you enter a room. Say, "hi," call his name, or stomp your feet. One owner makes a clicking noise with her tongue just before she picks up her small dog.

Changes in Barking Patterns

The most common bark is the canine call to arms. It is a way for one dog to tell the pack that danger approaches. Other barks initiate play, express joy, frustration, or inform us that the dog wants to go outdoors. Two interesting phenomena have been noted in blind dogs. Some dogs bark more than previously. Others bark less.

Blind dogs bark more when they are frustrated, insecure, or need your assistance. Some dogs sit, give a single bark, pause for a few seconds, and repeat. This may indicate that the dog needs you to help him get reoriented, open a door, or otherwise assist him.

In other cases, newly blind dogs bark less than they once did. Some owners speculate that this involves the survival-of-the-fittest concept. If a dog in the wild went blind (was weak) and he announced his whereabouts with a bark, he could be in danger of being attacked. Silence is a safety mechanism. Depression may also reduce barking.

Circling

Some dogs, especially the herding breeds, are famous for circling behaviors. Dogs commonly circle when their dinner is being prepared, when they need to go out, or before going for a walk. Blindness may increase circling behaviors in variety of ways. Some dogs will learn the lay of the land by circling and gently bumping into objects. In this way the dog memorizes the environment.

Disorientation causes many blind dogs to circle. This can occur when the dog wakens in a place he doesn't normally nap. The dog proceeds in ever-widening circles and appears to be searching for something familiar with which to orient himself. If he cannot find something familiar, the circling may become more frantic.

Owners can interrupt this behavior and help reorient the dog by leading him to a familiar spot. For one dog, this spot is the water bowl. For another, it may be the rug at the front door or his doggy bed. Some dogs use the sound of the television or radio to orient themselves. It can be helpful to leave these turned on when you leave the house.

Some blind dogs use circling as a way to exercise. Once they have memorized the layout of the house or yard, they may gleefully race around in circles. This is a safe way for them to burn off excess energy.

Circling may also have a physical cause. The pain of an ear infection, glaucoma, or other inflammation can cause a dog to circle. Circling can indicate that a seizure is imminent. Strokes and the high levels of cortisol — present in cases of SARD, Cushing's, and cognitive dysfunction — can cause slow, aimless circling.

Cats and Dogs

In many homes, cats become part of the domesticated dog pack. In others, they do not. Dogs may consider cats as prey and cats may consider dogs a threat. Correct the dog for chasing the cat. The water spray-bottle works well for this. Supervise your pets closely until they accept each other's presence.

If the cat wears a bell to save birds and you wish to put bells on the dogs in your pack, try to find some that sound different than the cat's bell. If the cat does not wear a bell, do not put one on her now.

Photo of blind Siberian Husky, "Jenilyn," courtesy of Jamie West

Sometimes it is the cat that torments the dog. This can be a dangerous situation since a blind dog is less able to avoid a claw scratch to the eye. Serious damage can result from such a scratch, sometimes requiring surgical repair. If the blind dog unwittingly and repeated stumbles upon your cat, it may be helpful to place a bell on the collar of the blind dog. In either case, it may be best if the cats can have one room as a dog-free zone. Brace the door partially closed or set a baby-gate at an angle to prevent large dogs from entering, while still leaving space for cats.

Remember that, as the true leader, it is your job to enforce good manners in your pack members. Remember, too, that a dog is more secure when he clearly knows his position in the pack. Consistent behaviors on your part will give your dog confidence.

TRAINING CONCEPTS

Some people wonder what value there is in training a blind dog. This is especially true if they haven't had much experience training dogs. These owners may believe that their dog is just a pet and doesn't require formal training.

Teaching blind dogs new skills has several important results. First, it is believed that dogs receiving formal training make a faster and better adjustment to blindness, compared to dogs that learn by trial and error. Second, when a dog learns new skills, he experiences success which builds confidence.

Photo of blind Golden Retriever, "Kate," courtesy of Garrie Stevens

As he learns new skills, the dog is able to function more as he did before the onset of blindness. Human blind patients refer to this as mobility training. They say it helps their self-esteem, their family relationships, and their general health.

Training sessions teach the dog that he can fight through his fears. In this way, it is possible to help a dog work through depression, apprehension, and dependency. Training new skills will give your dog something on which to focus. The result is a happier, more confident dog.

When dogs are able to continue with their daily activities (walking to the mailbox, riding in the car or boat), it contributes to their quality of life. Being included in these activities helps reduce a dog's anxiety and depression.

Training a blind dog is also a safety measure. Blind dog are at greater risk of injury from things unseen. This may include objects he bumps into, aggression from other dogs, or a moving motor vehicle. Training your dog to understand a few new commands may someday save his life.

Working with your dog is a wonderful way to spend time together. Blind-dog owners emphasize their role as the dog's coach and cheerleader. During the process of dog training, many beautiful human-canine bonds are forged. Training results in deeper trust and rapport. That being said, be alert if you take your dog to public obedience classes. Your dog may feel threatened by so many dogs he cannot see.

Positive Reinforcement

Volumes of literature have been written about canine behavior and training. In a nutshell, one way to train a dog is to give him a reward (such as a food treat) each time he performs the desired behavior. This is called positive reinforcement. Another way to train is by applying a correction or punishment when the desired behavior is not performed.

For our purposes, we will focus on training with positive reinforcement. Punishment has no place in working with blind dogs. Many of these dogs are already stressed or insecure. If they come to fear the training process because they have experienced punishment, it may hamper their progress. Fear of punishment will amplify aggressive and depressed behaviors.

"Leo," a blind Shih-Tzu

For most dogs, positive reinforcement translates to training with food. A food reward is the easiest way to tell a dog that he has correctly done what you've asked. Dogs, like humans, require a paycheck to maintain motivation in their work. If you are entirely against training with food, you can substitute your dog's favorite toy or verbal praise for the treat.

Working Through Stress

As you progress through the training process, be patient with your dog. If a dog does not perform the skill at first, it is usually because he does not understand what you are asking of him. This indicates that more practice, with rewards, is necessary. Experts believe it takes five repetitions in five different settings for a dog to learn a new skill.

If you believe that your dog does understand what you are asking of him, and he doesn't respond to you, it means he is stressed or worried about something else in the environment. In the past, trainers often thought that dogs were challenging their owners' authority when this occurred. Contemporary trainers believe this type of defiance rarely happens. You will notice stress, and have difficulty training, when new people come to your home or when you train in public.

If a dog does not perform a skill, he may not understand what you are asking of him.

Resist the temptation to verbally or physically chastise the dog during training. Collars will be used to communicate directional signals, but should not be used to give traditional collar pops or corrections. If you are unable to obtain the desired behavior, return to a simpler level of training.

The very clear presence of food treats held close to the dogs face will help him concentrate on what you are asking. Treats are also an effective way to lead or lure blind dogs.

Once the dog understands your commands and has succeeded in various settings, he will have learned that he can fight through stress and win a reward. After a number of repetitions (which varies from dog to dog) he will be able to follow your commands without food present.

At this point you may substitute verbal praise for food. The effectiveness of verbal praise also varies between dogs. Some individuals only require a "good boy," while others may need a "yippee!" accompanied by hand clapping. Be generous with your praise. It builds confidence.

If time passes and you feel your dog is not making progress, consider using a training technique called jackpotting. This term refers to rewarding the dog with multiple pieces of food. This helps many dogs work through stress.

Some dogs make slow progress due to physical causes. SARD dogs frequently exhibit signs of excess cortisol, the hormone released to soothe irritation. Cortisol is known for its damaging affects on the brain. It can hamper both learning ability and short-term memory. (See page 21 and page 159 for more detailed discussions of cortisol problems.)

If either you or the dog has a bad day, take a break from training and come back to it another time. Try to end each training session on a positive note.

Training Opportunities

Many people have busy schedules. If you believe you must set aside a particular time of day to train, it may never happen. Anytime can be training time. You can train your dog while you are waiting for the laundry to finish drying. You can train while you are waiting for dinner to cook. You can train during the commercial breaks of your favorite TV program.

Since training opportunities are present all day long, be prepared to take advantage of them. Some of the best training happens during moments of daily activities. Store training treats (dry treats such as freeze-dried liver, which won't spoil) in areas where you are trying to teach specific skills — near the staircase, for example.

Here, dried liver treats are kept in a decorative teacup.

There is one special effort you may have to make. Owners of multiple dogs find that they must separate the blind dog from other pack members in order to train. It is difficult to interact with a single dog, when other dogs are competing for training treats. Separate the dogs with a baby gate or put the others outdoors for a short time.

Choosing Verbal Commands

It is likely that your dog already understands a basic vocabulary. This might include such phrases as, "Do you want to go for a walk?" and "Dinner time!" The more you talk to your dog, the more he will understand.

It was once thought that dogs only had a capacity to understand about twenty words. Dog trainers realize that many dogs have vocabularies that are four, five, or even six times that size. Don't be afraid to talk to your dog. Many owners believe that their voice comforts their blind dogs.

As you teach the dog new skills, think about the words and phrases he already knows. Choose new vocabulary words that do not sound similar to other commands. This could cause the dog some confusion. The actual word or phrase is less important than how you use it. It is actually possible to train behaviors with the names of vegetables if you so desire! Choose commands that you can remember and will use consistently.

For example, if your dog already knows the word "Down" to mean, "Lie down," do not also use "Down" to mean "Take a step down the stairs." Choose another word, such as "Step" or "Curb." Give verbal commands in a pleasant and relaxed tone of voice. If you are frustrated to the point that it is showing up in your voice, take a break.

It's also valuable to have a word that informs the dog that he has completed the training exercise. This allows him to relax between moments of concentration. Dog trainers refer to this as *releasing* the dog. It does *not* mean to remove the leash and let him run free. Instead, use a word such as "Okay!" and clap your hands to let him know he has accomplished the task.

The importance of consistency cannot be overstated. This means consistent delivery and intonation of the commands, too. Much communication occurs through body language. For example, we lean over and point to the floor when we tell a dog to lie down. Since the blind dog cannot see this, verbal communication takes on greater importance. Help other members of the family deliver commands in the same way that you do.

With training, it is possible to recapture a number of behaviors lost with the onset of blindness. For example, if you miss the expression on your dog's face when you bring out a favorite toy, name the toy each time you give it to him. Remember, the more words you add to his vocabulary, the better. With time, the same look of anticipation may return. After all, most dogs, sighted or blind, come to learn the words "go for a walk." In fact, many owners must resort to spelling words in front of their dogs.

Training Equipment

Choosing training equipment for your dog is based on several factors: His size, energy level, and your strength. You may need to experiment with different types of equipment to learn which work best on your dog. As the dog's age and understanding of the training process change, so may the equipment.

Good examples of wide collars

Collars and Harnesses

Since much of our work will involve giving the dog directional cues by applying collar pressure, the choice of collar is important. For most indoor training, a wide collar is recommended. When cues are given with a wide collar, pressure is displaced and causes no discomfort.

Slip collars and choke chains are valuable for control, but are unnecessary for the type of positive reinforcement training recommended for blind dogs. In fact, during the training period,choke chains or slip collars are generally not recommended. Since these collars tighten and apply pressure all around the neck, the dog may consider this to be a correction. Choke chains may be necessary, however, in maintaining control outdoors. For small dogs, a body harness is another option.

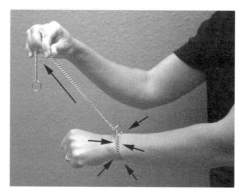

The advantage of a harness is that it transfers pressure cues over a larger portion of the dog's body. The disadvantage is that it generally does not offer as much control as a collar. Harnesses designed for carting have a D-ring at both sides of the harness. A leash can be connected between them to offer more control. Do not use anti-pull harnesses as they transfer pressure cues inappropriately. Head harnesses, or halters, can help owners lead high-energy dogs.

In some cases, a combination of equipment might be appropriate. For a large, energetic dog, a buckle collar or harness with one leash might be worn for training purposes, while a second leash with a choke chain, prong collar, or head halter provides control. While the prong collar may look harsh, it is in many ways more humane than other options. It offers superb control for strong dogs.

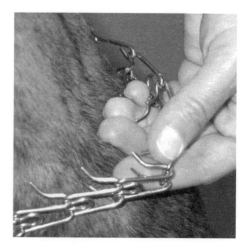

NOTE: In the wild, a bitch places her muzzle around a pup's face as a form of discipline. *Some* dogs react to facial pressure submissively. They may become depressed or avoid training sessions. If this occurs, switch back to a basic collar.

Leashes

Leashes made of chain link are not recommended. They are hard on your hands and they can hit the dog in the face. Use nylon, cotton, or leather leashes.

For indoor use, you will only need a short leash, perhaps three to six feet in length. For outdoor use, you may need a long line or retractable leash. The use of the pipe leash (plastic PVC plumbing pipe) will be discussed in the next chapter.

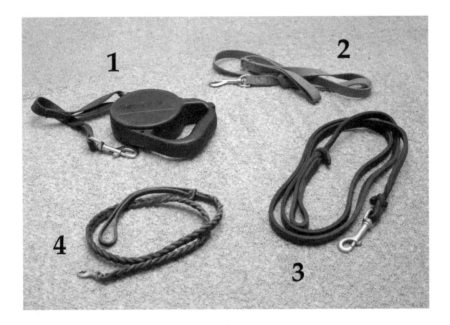

**Examples of good leashes: 1) retractable leash, 2) six-foot cotton leash,
3) six-foot leather leash, 4) three-foot braided leather leash**

NOTE: Take great care if you let your blind dog romp off lead. Many veterinarians do not recommend this. Your dog will be at a distinct disadvantage — and in possible danger — due to his vision loss.

Rewards

When you select treats for your dog, take into consideration food allergies or other health problems he might have. Also consider his calorie intake. Use smaller pieces for smaller dogs. If you are giving the dog large quantities of treats during training sessions, it may be necessary to cut back his dinner portions.

If your dog is a poor eater, choose foods that are palatable and aromatic. If your dog is still disinterested in food, try training just before his usual dinnertime. You may also use toys and verbal praise as rewards.

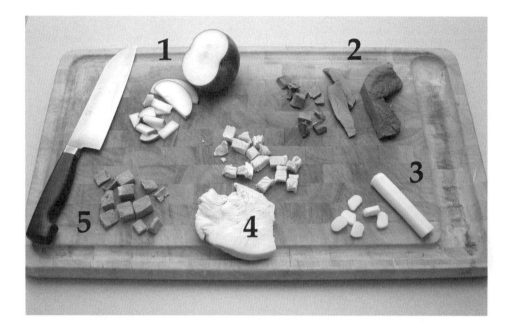

Examples of healthy training treats: 1) apple slices, 2) beef heart, 3) mozzarella string cheese, 4) turkey, 5) dehydrated liver

If your dog is *overly* excited by the presence of food, use treats that are a less interesting, such as apple or carrot slices. In these cases, train the dog *after* he has had his dinner. Experiment with different types of food to see which your dog likes, and which are easy to handle.

Other Equipment

Training treat bags are designed specifically for holding food treats. They may be purchased at pet supply stores or dog shows. Coats with large pockets work well, too! Since immediate rewards improve learning, plan on where you will keep your training treats.

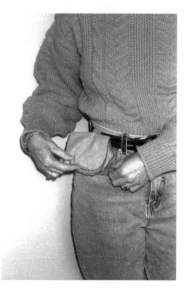

A wand or dowel can be useful when working with small dogs. Such training wands reduce the need to bend down. You will be able to give touch commands while standing.

Slowly introduce training equipment to your dog. This may include leashes, new collars, and the training wand. Some blind dogs are suspicious. Others have suffered abuse. Offer calm praise and food treats during the introduction.

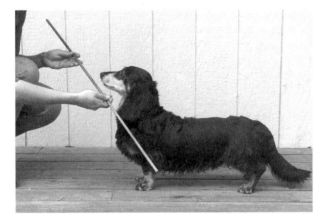 

References

Jecs, D., *Choose to Heel, the First Steps: An Innovative Dog Training Manual.* Puyallup, Washington: Self-published, 1995.

NEW SKILLS FOR BLIND DOGS

When a dog goes blind, he will need several new skills such as the *Go Slowly* (or *Easy)*, the *Wait*, the *Recall*, and the *Forward*. We will also discuss how to teach directional cues, managing steps, and other basic skills. Such training will improve your dog's adjustment to blindness.

The *Go Slowly* or *Easy*

One of the most important skills to teach your blind dog is to slow down on command. This allows you to help your dog avoid obstacles. It's also valuable to help your dog collect himself should he become disoriented.

Which actual word you choose to denote the command is less important than how you use it. Choose a word that you can draw out, such as "Slo-o-o-ow-ly", or "E-e-e-easy." Animals tend to slow down when they hear long, drawn-out sounds . . . which is exactly what you are asking him to do.

Teaching the *Go Slowly*

Initially, this can be taught indoors. You will need the dog to wear a buckle collar or a harness, and a leash. Move about the room with your dog. Do not call him to you because this will confuse him. If the dog just stands and waits for you to initiate activity, move this exercise outdoors where he will be more likely to move about.

When the dog has lost interest in you and is moving about, slow him down by gradually increasing tension on the leash, or by physically restraining him across his chest. Do not jerk the leash or hit him on the chest. Your attempts should not startle him into going slowly.

As you apply pressure to the leash or the dog, give a command, such as, "E-e-e-easy." Intonation is an important part of this exercise. The moment your dog slows, feed him a treat and praise him! If you signal the dog with tension from the leash, keep the treats in your other hand. If your use your hands to physically slow him, keep the food treats in your mouth or in a pocket that you can access quickly.

Release the dog from the exercise with "Okay" or similar word. Allow the dog to wander around again so that you may continue to practice.

Do not place an actual obstacle in front of the dog during training. It is important that he understands and responds to the command with confidence. If the dog failed to slow and he bumped into an obstacle, you would be training by punishment. It is important for the dog to trust you. A good pack leader would never knowingly set up his dog for failure.

Some dogs may come to a complete halt instead of merely slowing. At this point you might decide that the *Stop* is the skill better suited to your dog. See the following section for more details.

Other dogs may not stop or slow. In this case, hold a food treat slightly above his nose, but don't let him eat just yet. Lead him forward with the treat. Turn rather sharply toward your left. Proceed to make a small circle to the left. This will have the effect of blocking the dog's forward motion. As he slows, say the command and reward him for slowing.

Eventually, your dog will slow upon hearing the verbal command alone. The time frame for this can vary tremendously between dogs. Be patient. Continue to reward correct behavior. When your dog routinely slows on command, he is ready to practice this exercise off leash.

Teaching the *Go Slowly* Off Lead

You may practice without a leash in the house or fenced yard. Choose a time when your dog is calm or tired. If he is excited, he is more likely to bump into something once off leash. If this happens, place gentle pressure on his collar or chest, tap the obstacle with your hand, and repeat the command. While he is standing still, feed the dog a treat. By gently reminding the dog of what he was supposed to do, you will help him fight through distractions.

You will use this skill often. One owner explains that on her command of "Careful," the dog will slow down and prepare himself for *something*. This could mean a step, a wall, or furniture.

Watch your dog during his daily activities. If he's about to bump into an obstacle, give the command to go slowly. Then redirect him, remove the object, or call him in another direction. This is an exercise for which it is valuable to have treats located in convenient places around the house.

While this skill requires an effort on the owner's part, it can help overcome one of the elements people find most upsetting about canine blindness — watching their dog bump into objects. Be alert to your dog's whereabouts. Try to anticipate his movements and call out verbal cues as needed.

The *Stop* or *Wait*

Some owners teach their dogs the distinction between slowing and coming to a complete stop. The *Stop* or *Wait* is valuable if you need to pick up an obstacle, move it out of the way, or when your dog is loose and you wish to re-leash him.

The *Wait* is also useful when the dog is preparing to jump off the couch or out of the car and you want to control his leap. Use this command when your dog is disoriented or needs assistance in another part of the house. In this way, he will know what to do until you come and help him.

As you and your dog work together, you can decide if you need to train one or both of these commands. However, do not teach these exercises simultaneously. The *Go Slowly* and *Stop* may seem different to us, but teaching them together could be confusing for the dog.

Teaching the *Stop* or *Wait*

In training the *Wait*, you will use a different command and intonation from that used for the *Go Slowly*. Whereas the *Go Slowly* command is long and drawn-out, the *Wait* command is short and sharp, such as, "Stop!" or "Wait!" It is not necessary, however, to yell.

Gradual pressure should be applied to the leash or chest until the dog comes to a complete stop. Do not yank or jerk the leash. Reward the dog when he comes to a stop. Feed several treats so he remains still. Then release him.

The *All Clear*

One blind-dog owner feels it is valuable to have a word to signify the opposite of *Wait*. She trusts her dog off leash and in safe, wide-open spaces she tells the dog that it's "All Clear" to run. The dog understands that in this situation there are no obstacles near.

Again, take great care if you let your blind dog romp off lead. He will be at a disadvantage with vision loss. A good compromise between safety and freedom is the use of long lines or retractable leashes.

The *Come When Called* or *Recall*

While this may not actually be a new skill for your dog, it is a skill worth reviewing. If your dog did not come when called as a sighted dog, it will be especially valuable to retrain this skill. The *Recall* can bring your dog to you if he becomes disoriented in the yard, as a means of play, and can remove him from harm's way.

Traditionally, the *Recall* is taught by calling the dog's name, followed by the word "Come!" If the dog does not obey, many professional dog trainers encourage the owner to go to the dog and physically or verbally correct him. They even recommend dragging the dog toward you. These dogs are quickly conditioned to view the *Recall* as a thoroughly unpleasant exercise.

If your dog has had such an experience, you will have to work a little harder to undo what has already been done. Do not fear. It can be done. Choose a new phrase to help the dog start over with this exercise. Try using the word, "Here," for example.

Teaching the *Recall* — Part One

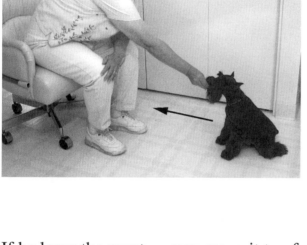

Hold a training treat up to your dog's nose, at arm's length. Your dog need not start in the sitting position, as with the formal obedience exercise. *Slowly* draw your hand toward your body. Move slowly so the dog moves with the treat. If your dog stops, move the treat back to his nose and continue to lure him forward with it.

If he loses the scent — you move it too fast for him — he may start hunting around for the treat. Try to prevent this. We are trying to teach him to come toward you as directly as possible.

**Lure the dog back toward you
if he becomes distracted.**

When the dog gets close to you, feed him the treat and give him verbal praise. Tell him he what a good dog he is! The dog need not sit when he reaches you, either. Release him and repeat.

Once you have practiced this a number of times, the dog should realize that following a piece of food toward you results in him getting that treat. Since we will eventually be adding an element of distance to the *Recall*, we now need to give the dog another cue in addition to the scent.

Teaching the *Recall* — Part Two

Now we will add a continuous sound to the exercise. This could be the command repeated over and over, such as "Come-come-come-come," or "Puppy-puppy-puppy." This continuous sound will act as an auditory guide when the dog is far from you.

In addition to using your voice, you may also clap your hands or use a squeaky toy, whistle, or clicker. (Clickers are used in some forms of obedience training. See *Suppliers* section.) The only drawback to using these items comes when you misplace them!

Work in an open area. Move the furniture out of the way, if necessary. An unexpected bump may cause the dog to become suspicious of this exercise. Be careful about calling your dog in situations that put his safety at risk.

Teaching the *Recall* — Part Three

Once your dog is comfortable working with food and the continuous sound, it is time to add the element of distance to the exercise. Step back from the dog, extend the treat at arms length, and begin your continuous sound. If the dog does not move in your direction (doesn't move at all or moves in the wrong direction), step up to him, place the treat under his nose, and slowly guide him toward you.

As your practice sessions continue, gradually add more distance. When the dog can find your hand from two feet away with the continuous sound, extend the distance to three feet. Progress slowly.

The owners of small dogs believe that squatting down can also be helpful. They believe the sound reaches the dog more directly. The owners of SARD dogs report that transient (non-permanent) hearing loss and confusion are common. Attempts to lower cortisol production can be helpful in these cases.

Eventually the dog will follow your voice toward your hand and then follow your hand toward you. Always feed the dog when he gets to you. Never scold or shake the dog if he is slow in coming. It will make matters worse.

If your dog is suddenly unable to find you and seems disoriented, you may have moved too far, too soon. Return to practicing at a closer distance until the dog's confidence and understanding improve. Eventually, your dog should come to your continuous sound from across the room.

Teaching the *Recall* — Part Four

Next, move this exercise outdoors. This is an *enormous* change for the dog. There are abundant sounds and scents, which make it much harder for the dog to concentrate. Start at the beginning.

In a secure area, such as a fenced yard, start with the dog following the treat from arm's length with your continuous sound. You will gain a feel for how loud you will need to make your continuous sound to be heard outdoors. Gradually add distance to the exercise. Continue to reward with food. It may take a number of practice sessions to gain the same results you experienced indoors. This is normal.

If the dog fails to come to you because he is distracted, walk up to him. (Do not frighten him or scold him.) Position the treat under his nose and draw him toward you. When he reaches you, feed and praise him.

After the dog has learned this exercise to your satisfaction, continue to randomly reinforce it with food rewards. For example, reward the dog when he comes when called from the yard. Keep a container of treats near the door. Owners of deaf dogs also suggest adding vibration to this exercise. This may include stomping your feet or training with a vibrating collar. (See Chapter 14, *Dogs Both Blind and Deaf*.)

Managing Steps and Stairs

Steps and stairs can be challenging for blind dogs. Owners typically say that going down stairs is harder for their dogs than going up stairs. They believe their dogs worry if the next stair tread really exists or not. Remember that blind dogs may experience an element of fear while learning this exercise. Be patient with them.

Until such time that your dog has mastered these skills, block off the staircases in your house and yard. With some dogs, such as Dachshunds and small, toy breeds, it may be best to avoid stairs, sighted *or* blind. While it is important not to coddle a blind dog, it is realistic that some dogs will need to be carried up and down stairs or taught to use ramps.

Dogs, unlike humans, have a wonderful mental ability called cognitive mapping. They are able to maintain a mental picture of their territory. This skill is valuable to wild dogs and wolves. It enables them to find their dens and locate the hidden remains of prey within many miles of territory.

Photo of blind Border Collie, "Allie," courtesy of Olivia Bravo

Most blind dogs develop a remarkably good mental map of their environment. Until that map is developed though, there are extra cues you can provide a blind dog to help him get around. Once the dog has adjusted, you may eliminate the training aids.

If your dog has a little vision, choose some type of tape that will contrast in color with the steps. For light colored steps, use black electrical tape. For dark steps, use masking tape. The high contrast may help low-vision dogs notice the height of the step. If the dog is completely blind, the fresh tape may provide him with a scent cue. Replace the tape at the start of each practice session so the scent is fresh.

The edges of these concrete steps have been painted to provide contrast.

Also, choose commands you will be comfortable using in public. Do not select a command such as "Down" for stepping down if your dog already responds to "Down" as lie down. Some choices might include, "Up," "Curb," "Step," or "Stairs." Some owners use the same command for climbing up and down steps. Others make the distinction with different terms.

It is not necessary to use a leash when teaching this exercise. Choose a place in your house with a minimum of steps. One step is best to start. Find a place where the dog will have enough room to stand both below the step and above it. In some homes this means being creative, such as using a railroad tie in the landscaping. In time, you will need to find a set of two or three steps, and later, a short flight of stairs on which to practice.

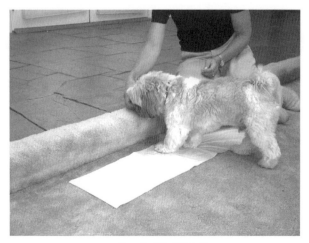

"Leo," a blind Shih-Tzu

Teaching Steps and Stairs — Going Up — Part One

Start by training the dog to go up stairs, since this is a typically easier for the dog and will give him confidence. Apply contrasting tape at the top of the vertical side (the riser of each step).

With a food treat, lead your dog to the bottom of the single step. Tap the top of the step with your hand. If the dog is tall enough to eat off of the step, lead his nose to the top of the step and place the food there. Verbally encourage him to eat it by saying, "Get It!" The height of the food gives him some spatial information about the step.

After several repetitions, begin placing the food a little farther back from the edge of the step. Progress slowly, a few inches at a time. Each time, tap near the food and encourage him to get it.

Eventually, the food will be far enough from the edge of the step that the dog cannot reach it without taking a step up.

As he hops up the step, give your command.
Reward him with several extra treats and lavish verbal praise. It may be necessary to assist a smaller dog. Place his forepaws on the tread of the step each time you put down the treat.

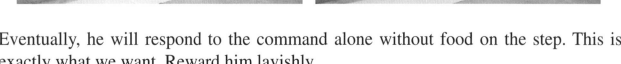

Eventually, he will respond to the command alone without food on the step. This is exactly what we want. Reward him lavishly.

Teaching Steps and Stairs — Going Up — Part Two

Locate a place that has two or three steps. Tap the first step and let him eat from it. Next, give your command. The goal is to get him to place his front feet on the step. Since he has already learned to hop up, it may be necessary to catch him (restrain him with your hand across his chest or tell him "Wait,") so that he doesn't stumble up the rest of the steps.

Place a treat on top of the *second* step, tap the step, and encourage him eat it. Move the food treat further back from the edge. Eventually, the dog will need to climb both steps in order to reach the treat. As he does, repeat your command. Reward him with treats and lavish praise.

Practice this several times. Next, eliminate the piece of food resting on the first step, give your command for each step, and reward him when he reaches the top. Now he is ready to try a small flight of stairs.

The principles are exactly the same. The goal is to get the dog to place his forepaws on each succeeding stair tread. Reward him each time he does this. His back legs will follow. If he has trouble, return to an earlier level of training for several sessions or take a break from training for a few days.

Teaching Steps and Stairs — Going Down — Part One

Retraining the dog to go down steps may require a little more patience and ingenuity on your part. Some blind dogs are frightened of stepping down. The dog must trust that you are not asking him to walk off a cliff. If your dog shows significant signs of stress (panting, growling, or avoidance), proceed in very small increments. While it may be scary to the dog at first, it can be a tremendous confidence builder once achieved.

Return to the location where you trained on the single step. This time, apply the contrasting tape along the edge of the horizontal side of the step (the tread).

To prepare the dog for this new exercise, lead him *up* the step, first. This will reinforce his awareness of the height of the step.

Using the food, lure his nose to the tape strip. Place the treat at the edge of the step and encourage him to eat it. Repeat several times.

After eating several treats, your dog should start to relax. Scratch him behind the ears and rub him on the chest. For a small- to medium-size dog, slide your hand under his chest, lift his front feet off the ground, move him forward a few inches, and carefully set his forepaws down at the bottom of the step. As you set him down, say your command. Immediately give him a food treat.

If he stays in that position, lure him forward with a treat.

Teaching Steps and Stairs — Going Down — Part Two

If the dog is uncomfortable with this strategy or if the dog is too large to lift, there is another approach. Leave the step. Return to the center of the room. Place a sheet of notebook paper or newspaper on the floor. Using a food treat as lure, draw his head down to the paper. Place the treat on the paper and encourage him to eat it. Repeat, but drop the treat from a height of about six inches from the paper. Encourage him to find it.

The dropped treat should make a distinct noise. Between the noise and the scent, your dog should be able to locate it. If he is confused, lead his nose down to the paper with another treat.

Continue dropping the treat onto the paper from gradually increasing heights. Ultimately, you should be able to drop a treat from the height of your dog's head, and he should be able to find it.

Allow the dog to experience stepping on to the paper. Make sure the newspaper is smooth so the treat actually stays where it lands. If this becomes a problem, experiment with other materials like aluminum foil or a sheet of plastic.

Now return to the single-step-down exercise. Warm up the dog by asking him to hop up the step. Position your dog at the top of the step and tell him to "Wait." Place the piece of paper at the bottom of the step.

With a treat in your hand, draw your dog's head down a few inches and drop the treat on the paper. The combination of the sound and the mental picture of the step (the warm-up exercise) will give the dog courage to step down and get the treat.

If your dog continues to have trouble, try the exercise just prior to mealtime when your dog might be his hungriest. Continue working on the drop-the-food-on-paper exercise separately from practicing the step. And continue to train the dog to go *up* steps.

Make sure you are training in a calm and pleasant voice. Never push or trick the dog into taking a step downward. Owners report that this is a difficult skill to teach their blind dogs. Slow progression is normal. Keep trying.

The first time your dog steps down on his own, lavish him with praise and reward him with treats. Tell him what a brave and wonderful dog he is! Repeat until your dog is stepping down regularly each time you drop the treat and give the command.

Teaching Steps and Stairs — Going Down — Part Three

Once the dog steps down on command, you can progress to a set of two or three stairs. The progression of stepping down two stairs is much like it was for climbing up two stairs. The goal is to reward the dog every time he responds to your command and sets his front paws down on another step.

To warm up, have the dog climb up two or three steps. Lure the dog around and ask him to step down. You may need to use the paper at the bottom of each step. Be prepared to steady him in case he stumbles.

It is possible that simply tapping the step may be a sufficient cue. When your dog is relaxed and comfortable with this exercise, move on to a short flight of stairs. Reward every step downward. Practice on all the stairs around your house. Remember the golden rule of dog training — five repetitions in five different settings are necessary for a new behavior to become ingrained.

One owner counts down the stairs in a singsong voice. He calls out the number of steps in descending order, such as, "Six, five, four, three, two, one!" And he calls them out in a descending scale of notes. It is certainly conceivable that dogs can understand that they are coming to the last step when they hear, "Three, two, one!" Another owner stomps her foot until the dog has reached the bottom.

In time, most blind dogs will be able to master stairs. One dog owner reports that, initially, her dog lay down and reached out to feel the next stair tread. Another owner says that her dog gained exceptional confidence. Now, the dog just feels for the top step with his paw and clears the remaining three in a single bound!

Alternatives to Stairs

Occasionally, a dog will have significant difficulty with stairs. He may be timid or in poor health. The steps might be exceptionally steep. In these cases, other options should be considered.

Help large, elderly dogs, by slipping a towel under their belly to act as a sling. You can also use a canvas log-carrier (the type found in fireplace stores), as they are often made with handles. Pet slings are available commercially. (See *Suppliers* section.) Small dogs may be carried. Keep the stairs closed-off with a baby gate in these situations.

Another option is to build a ramp. Ramps are easier for blind individuals to navigate because feet need not be placed in any specific spot. Ramps also reduce the amount of jarring that geriatric joints must endure.

Enlist the skills of an experienced carpenter or purchase a commercial dog ramp. It would be detrimental to the dog's self-confidence if the ramp collapsed under him. Tack down anti-skid tape or outdoor carpeting. A safety railing will prevent the dog from accidentally walking off the side.

Teaching the Dog to Use a Ramp

With a treat, lure the dog to the bottom of the ramp. Dab bits of peanut butter, cream cheese, or other soft food up the ramp. Encourage him to get each succeeding treat. Praise him as he advances. It may take several practice trips before he has a mental map of the ramp's location and use.

Walking a Blind Dog on Leash

Some dogs have little experience walking on leash. Others have suffered abuse and fear the leash and collar. Since the benefits of exercise are significant, it is worth the effort to leash train all dogs.

If the dog rolls over when you attempt to attach the leash, have training treats available in the area where you leash-up. Place a training treat in front of his nose. He will likely flip over in an attempt to eat it. As he does so tell him, "Stand." If he does not flip over, verbally encourage him to "Get it!" Feed him once he is standing.

You may be able to attach the leash now. Have a second training treat in your hand and attach the leash while he is eating. In time, he will become more confident during the leashing procedure. The food will teach him that staying upright is a rewarding experience.

If the dog fears the collar, leave it on the floor where the dog will be able to pass it and sniff it. Next, have it in your hand and allow the dog sniff it. Immediately feed the dog a treat.

Advance the exercise by touching the collar to the dog's side and feeding a treat. Touch it to his neck and reward. Lay it across the back of his neck and reward. You may need a partner to feed him while you buckle the collar. Offer verbal praise as you progress.

If the dog fears the leash, purchase a bolt snap at the hardware store and tie a short length of cord to it. This need only be long enough for the dog to feel a bit of weight, but not long enough on which to trip. You may also purchase a training tab (a short four- to six-inch leash).

Introduce this tiny leash to your dog as described above until you are able to attach it to his collar. Allow him to wear this around the house for several days. Gradually replace it with longer or heavier pieces of cord, or a very short leash. Reward and praise the dog. Remove collars and leashes at the end of each day, prior to bedtime.

Once the dog has accepted the short leash, pick up the end of it, feed him a treat, and gently let it go again. Next, pick up the leash and hold if for a few seconds longer. Reward the dog during the time you are holding the leash, since that is the activity you wish to promote.

By this point, dogs are usually relaxing with this exercise, and realizing that the leash isn't so bad after all. Without placing pressure on the collar, lure the dog forward with a training treat held to his nose.

As you continue, occasionally allow the dog to feel pressure from the leash. It doesn't matter how you exert the pressure (forward, backward, etc.), but rather, that the dog feels some pressure and realizes that everything is still all right. Praise and release the dog. Switch to a standard-length leash. Introduce any other training tools in the same fashion just described.

The *Forward*

Blindness can make some dogs hesitant to go for a walk. Sometimes the cause is physical. SARD dogs experience daytime lethargy which is likely related to excess cortisol production. This symptom can be minimized in many dogs with dietary measures. In other dogs, the hesitancy is due to fear. Teaching the *Forward* can help alleviate this.

Teaching the *Forward*

Hold a food treat close to his nose. For small dogs, try placing peanut butter on a long, wooden spoon. Walk forward slowly and talk to him excitedly. Tell him "Forward!" as he moves. Allow the dog to nibble and lick the treat, but do not give it to him until he has trotted for four or five steps.

Practice the *Forward* on a wide open, level surface so the dog will trust you. As trust develops, increase your pace. Next, use the food treat as a reward, instead of a lure. Do not hold the food directly to his nose this time. Give your command and if the dog trots forward, reward him. If he does not trot forward upon command, return to the previous step.

The Pipe-Leash

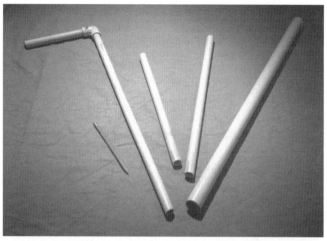

Blind dogs benefit from a little guidance when they are walked on leash. They need help knowing when to step up or down and how to avoid objects. This can be accomplished with both verbal commands and by touch cues.

The best tactile, or touch, cues will consist of pressure to help guide the dog. Since this is difficult to accomplish with a standard leash, a slight modification is recommended. The primary consideration is that the leash be stiff enough to help steer the dog.

A simple and inexpensive way to steer the dog is by purchasing a length of plastic PVC plumbing pipe and threading your leash through it. It is best when the pipe's diameter is small enough that you can wrap your hand around it, but large enough for you to thread the leash through. If the bolt snap is too large to fit through the pipe, try threading the handle end of the leash into the pipe. If that fails, purchase a thinner leash with a smaller snap.

Cut the pipe length so that you can carry your hand in a comfortable position. Experiment with different lengths and diameters. With a little ingenuity, these pipes can even be fashioned with a handle by attaching an elbow piece or wrapping the top of the pipe in foam rubber. One owner even threads the leash through his aluminum walking cane.

Another option is to construct a stick-leash. Purchase a wooden dowel and an inexpensive leash. Cut off the bottom portion of the leash to include the snap and about four inches of leash. Securely tape this piece to the end of the dowel. If yours is a high-energy dog, purchase a thick dowel. Screw a round eye bolt into one end. You will also need to purchase a double-ended snap to connect the eye bolt to the dog's collar.

Use a harness or wide collar to steer the dog. If you are using a carting harness with side D-rings, fashion a U-shaped PVC handle similar to the harnesses used on guide dogs for blind humans.

Avoid slip collars or choke chains that tighten around the dog's neck. They will not provide directional cues. Some dogs may interpret a tight collar as a correction for disobedience.

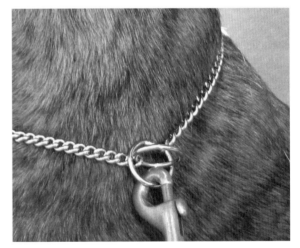

If you have an uncontrollable dog, consider using the choke chain with the leash attached to the dead ring (the ring that does not pull the collar tight). This will provide control while still transferring pressure cues appropriately.

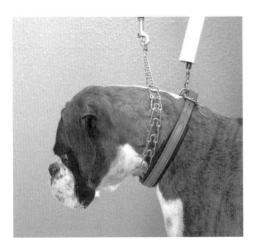

If you need additional control, add a separate collar and leash. For example, try a buckle collar to steer and a choke chain or prong collar for control. Such two-leash arrangements may become unnecessary as the dog matures or develops a better understanding of the "Go Slowly" command.

If you are unable to manage the two-leash arrangement, exercise the dog before you go for a walk. Try to tire him by playing games in the yard or house.

Teaching the Dog Directional Cues

Choose new vocabulary words that you will use to teach your dog to move from side to side. Appropriate phrases include, "Move Over," "This Way," or "That Way." Some owners use only one term and rely on pressure cues to indicate direction.

Other owners choose separate terms to indicate right and left. If you choose the latter, try the commands used by dog-sled mushers ("Gee," which means right, and "Haw," which means left) or those used by herders ("Away," which you can use to mean left, and "Go By," which you can use to mean right).

Teaching Directional Cues — Part One

To start, teach the directional cues indoors where fewer distractions are present. Once the dog has learned the basics indoors, you can progress outside. Be patient as you try this. Sideways movement is not a very natural thing for the dog. Be gentle and praise any sideways movement instantly.

Stand next to your dog, as if you were taking a walk. With the pipe-leash attached to the dog's collar or harness, apply three short presses to push the dog away from your side. If the dog does take a step away from you, say your command. Reward and praise him *immediately.*

The pressure should come in short bursts. The reason for this is that dogs possess an oppositional reflex. This refers to the dog's tendency to push back when something pushes against him. If you apply long, steady pressure, the dog may push back toward you. Keep the taps of pressure short.

Teaching Directional Cues — Part Two

If your dog does not move away after giving him the cues, turn 90 degrees and face the side of your dog's body. Gently and carefully walk into your dog. (Take a step toward the dog.)

The idea is *not* to frighten the dog into moving. If your dog thinks of you as the leader he will oblige you by moving out of your way. Small dogs are especially conscious of staying clear of human feet. As he moves away, say your command and reward him.

Repeat this exercise until he moves away with only the collar taps. Work on only one direction per training session.

Teaching Directional Cues — The Small Dog

If your small dog is fearful of your moving feet, use a training wand to gently tap the dog. This wand can be a thin wooden dowel, the plastic rod used to close Venetian blinds, or a telescoping pointer. The wand is also helpful for dogs that move only their front feet. With a wand, you can teach the dog that he should move his hindquarters, too.

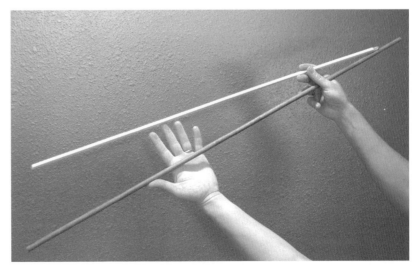

If the dog moves only his front feet, do reward that movement. In addition, gently tap his haunches with the wand, repeat your command and heavily reward his movement. With practice, the dog should start moving both parts of his body together.

Teaching Directional Cues — The Large Dog

Steer large and giant dogs with pressure cues (hand contact) along the dog's sides. One owner places her palm on the dog's far side and nudges him close to her as they pass through doorways. Another owner places her palm against her dog's side and pushes his fur upward to direct him up a flight of stairs. Large dogs may lean against you to get directional cues. This helps him know where you are going.

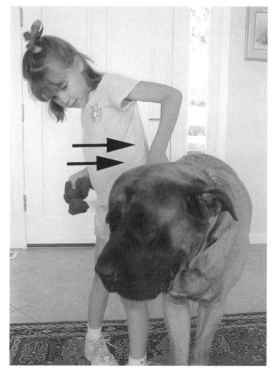

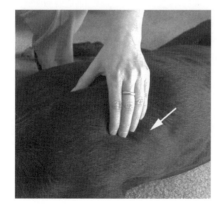

Putting It All Together

The goal of this combined training is to be able to walk with your dog and steer him to the right or left as needed. In this way, you will be able to keep him from walking off the curb, into potholes, and other obstacles. If your dog has vision in one eye, position the dog so that his blind eye is nearer to you. Steer him clear of your feet.

It will be *your job* to stay alert and scan for terrain changes and upcoming dangers. Keep alert for twigs and bushes that could poke your dog's face. Realize that even small obstacles — a crack in the sidewalk — may trip small dogs. Remember that you are now his seeing-eye-*person*.

Some owners take a lesson from guide dogs trained for blind humans! When the owner comes to a step, not only does he give the *Go Slowly* and *Step* commands to his dog, but comes to a stop himself. This gives the dog an opportunity to complete the maneuver without being left behind.

The same is true if you are steering the dog sideways. Slow down or stop while the dog is side stepping. If you were to keep walking, the dog would be left behind since he is not making forward motion.

Stay alert for obstacles that may cause your dog trouble: (1) electrical box covers, (2) shrubbery branches, (3) trees and sign posts.

Also, watch for (1) changes in elevation, (2) sewer grates, (3) potholes or cracks in the pavement.

Additional Aides

If you need to handle a very large dog, you may wish to forego the leash entirely. It is possible to purchase handsome leather collars with a rigid, built-in handle. This permits you to give instant cues to your dog, which is valuable in tight quarters, such as the veterinarian's office.

Dogs that handle themselves well on leash may progress to long lines or retractable leashes. Long lines were originally designed for tracking. They are constructed of cotton and nylon web or polypropylene cord. These are commercially available in lengths from 15- to 40-feet long.

Polypropylene cord is exceptionally lightweight and is available at hardware stores in various diameters. Avoid tangles with these long lines though, as they can trip the dog or cause friction burns on both of you.

The invention of the retractable leash combines the freedom of the long line with the control and safety of a short leash. Most dog owners are familiar with these plastic encased leashes that unroll as the dog moves away from the handler and rewind when the dog returns. They are available in lengths from seven to 32 feet.

Use the *Go Slowly* or *Easy* when you ask the dog if he wants to go for a walk. (Many dogs spin and hit obstacles in their excitement.) Use a calm tone of voice when you ask him this.

Use the *Go Slowly* or *Easy* when the dog is moving quickly and is about to hit the end of the leash. Use this command (or use the *Wait* command) when he is in danger of walking into an obstacle. Be certain that your dog responds to directional cues on the standard leash before progressing to long leashes.

Other Basic Skills

Blind-dog owners teach the *Sit* by placing gentle pressure or taps on the dog's hindquarters. Use a food treat to lure his head backward. Say, "Sit" as he does so.

The *Down* can be taught by laying your forearm along the dog's back while luring his head to the ground with a treat. Give the command "Down." Try not to give the dog two messages at once, such as "Puppy, just sit down." Reward him during the training phase and occasionally thereafter to keep the exercise reliable.

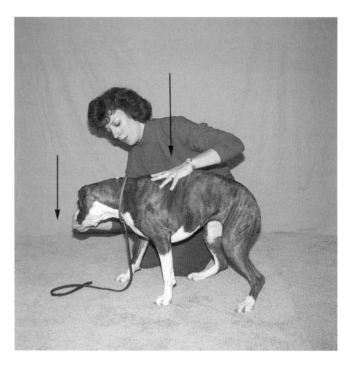

Stays should be taught on leash. Place the dog in a sit or down. Pull the leash gently, while simultaneously holding your hand against the dog's chest or back. Experiment to learn which one keeps him in place. Steady pressure on the leash will activate your dog's oppositional reflex. The dog should resist the pressure and stay where he is. After a few seconds, tell the dog "Good stay."Reward and release him.

**Activate the dog's oppositional reflex
in both the sit and the down positions.**

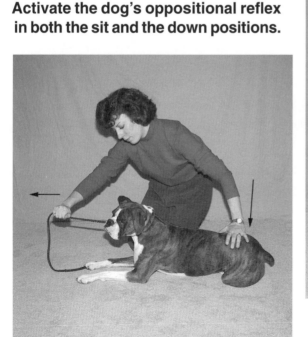

Gradually increase both the length of time you pull on the leash and the distance you stand from the dog. Should the dog get up and come to you, return to a shorter length of time or stand closer to the dog. Do not punish the dog for coming to you. Remember, some blind dogs experience a greater degree of separation anxiety. Your goal is to build your dog's confidence. If he gets up, it simply means he is stressed or doesn't yet understand what you are asking of him.

Applying Eye Drops

The stays are valuable skills if you need to give your dog eye drops. It may be necessary to give your dog eye drops in a variety of situations and it can be helpful to practice your technique before attempting to actually medicate your dog.

If your dog is wearing an Elizabethan cone/collar, remove it during the procedure. Let your dog nibble on a food treat. While he nibbles, approach the dog from behind. Stand by his side or straddle his back if possible.

Massage and pet your dog's head and neck. With the eye drop bottle in your dominant hand, reach around to steady the dog's head between both hands, and tilt his muzzle slightly upward. Quickly pull down the lower lid and pretend to express a drop.

You may stop and offer him a food treat or continue on. Move your hands to the other side of his face and repeat. If yours is a highly active dog, move quickly. If you are straddling him, try to steady him between your legs.

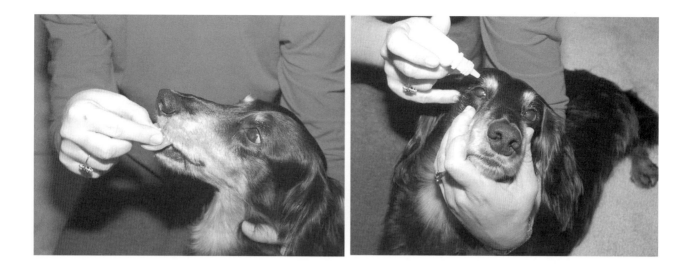

Reassuring comments may also prove helpful. Some dog owners keep a food treat close to the dog's face, either on a low table or chair, or have a family member hold it nearby. A final option, odd as it may sound, is to spread a small amount of peanut butter or cream cheese on the refrigerator door. This will distract the dog, as well as help keep his head elevated.

Another method of applying eye drops involves having the dog lie down on his side. This places his eye on a very flat plane, and even if he blinks, the drop should fall onto the surface of the eye when he opens his lid. Of course, if both eyes require medication, you will need to position him twice, once on each side. Lure him into position with a food treat. Give the position a name such as "on your side."

Reward him each time he gets into position. Gently cup your hand over his eye following administration, if he has a tendency to paw at his face.

> NOTE: Drops are more comfortable when they are room temperature. If your drops are refrigerated, hold the bottle in your fist for several minutes before administration.

Ongoing Training

If you are having difficulty teaching your dog the skills mentioned herein, see page184 for additional resources. *New Skills for Blind Dogs,* a companion film to this chapter, may help you better understand and teach these exercises.

It is likely that you will find a need for your dog to learn other basic skills particular to your environment and way of life. Examples might include going through a doggy-door, jumping into the car, or maneuvering at the veterinarian's office. Many of these will be covered in the next few chapters.

If you find the need to teach your dog a skill not covered in this book, follow the theories outlined in chapters seven and eight. The key to successful dog training is to break down each skill into small pieces of behavior. Reward exactly the behavior that you want the dog to retain. Give the new behavior a name and use it consistently.

When the dog is comfortable with one small piece, add another small behavior. Eventually you will have taught your dog a string of behaviors, which will result in a new skill.

References

Jecs, D., *Choose to Heel, the First Steps*: *An Innovative Dog Training Manual.* Puyallup, Washington: Self-published, 1995.

Jerison, H., *The Evolution of the Brain and Intelligence.* Academic Press, 1973.

MacDonald, D.W., *Running With the Fox*, London: Unwin Hyman Press, 1987.

NEGOTIATING THE HOUSE

Many blind dogs develop an excellent mental map of their environment. Until that map is developed, there are certain things you can do to help your dog adjust. Once the dog has made this adjustment you may eliminate many of the training aids that are mentioned below.

Minimizing Dangers

Look around your house. Are there things that could harm your dog: Things he might trip over, fall into, or knock down? Remind children to pick up their toys. If the dog is bumping into tables, remove glass objects that might topple on top of him.

Lighting

In some cases, especially with night blindness, better lighting may improve vision. Halogen bulbs are recommended as they provide a whiter, brighter light. Leave a light on in areas that the dog frequents: The hallway, porch, or dog run. This is especially true if your dog can let himself out of the house through a doggy door.

Human patients with low vision explain that there is a fine line between the benefits of bright light and the problem of glare. In certain cases, especially with cataracts, glare can cancel out the benefits of bright light. Experiment with lighting to see what works best for your dog. In cases of progressive blindness, there often comes a point where bright lighting no longer helps.

Using Contrast

Contrast refers to marking important locations with shades of black and white. If your dog has retained a small amount of vision, contrast marking may be valuable for the duration of his life.

If you've been training your dog to manage steps and stairs, you are already familiar with marking the edges of the steps with contrasting tape. Likewise, you may mark other areas of the house that cause the dog trouble, such as wall corners and doorjambs.

Once you've marked the trouble areas, watch your dog. As he moves nearer the place you have marked, give the "Go Slowly" command. You may even tap the wall with your hand. If your dog has retained vision, he will come to understand that the high contrast marks mean that he should slow down.

E-e-easy

Other items to mark with high contrast include:
- the dog's food and water bowls
- bedding or his safe spot
- mats placed in front of the doggy door
- mats placed in front of steps

Scent Marking

Scent marking is a highly recommended method of assisting a blind dog, especially one that is totally blind. With this method, it is possible to capitalize on a dog's outstanding olfactory (smelling) abilities. Experts differ markedly in their estimations of the canine's scenting ability but it is safe to say that it is far greater than that of any human.

Scents can be used in two ways. They can help your dog *find* important locations in your home or they can help him *avoid* obstacles. First, decide which scents are preferred in your household. This is especially important if family members suffer from allergies.

The scents that last the longest are those with oil bases. This includes high-quality perfumes (not colognes, which are water based) and scented oils for potpourri. These oils are available at bath shops, craft stores, and beauty-supply shops.

Scented oils, also called essential oils, are available in a wide variety of fragrances such as floral, citrus, herbal, and woody (pine, cypress, juniper, etc.). The citrus scents seem to be less offensive to allergy sufferers. Avoid rosemary and pine fragrances if your dog suffers from seizures.

Oil-based products need to be reapplied every week or two. Once the dog has developed his mental map of the house, it may be unnecessary to reapply them at all.

Other options include air fresheners, body deodorants, and furniture polishes. These are available in aerosol spray cans. Air fresheners are also available as candles and in small pots. These can be placed on the corners of low tables. Also consider ingredients from the kitchen, such as vanilla or almond extract.

Scent areas that are significant to the average dog. Examples include his safe spot, water bowl area, and the door to the yard. Scent each one with a different fragrance. Marking these important areas will help the dog build his mental map.

If you don't wish to apply the scent directly to an item, apply the oil onto felt fabric dots used to protect floors from furniture scratches. These dots have a tape backing which can be applied to the item you wish to mark. Flavored dental floss can also be tied around objects.

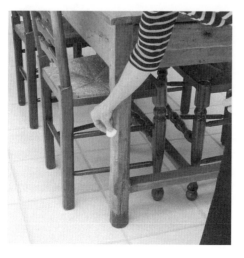

If your dog repeatedly bumps into an obstacle, such as a doorjamb or coffee table, scent that item with a fourth fragrance. However, choose only a *few* important areas. Too many scents might be confusing for the dog. Also, apply these scents sparingly. It is believed that scents applied too strongly are overwhelming.

Teaching the Dog to Understand Scent Marking

Many dogs need little or no formal training for this cue. They quickly come to associate a particular scent with an item. If your dog continues to bump into furnishings after you have scented them, practice the *Go Slowly* exercise as he nears a troublesome spot.

As the dog approaches the obstacle, tap the spot with your hand and give the command. Reward him for slowing. He should come to associate the scent with the need to slow down.

Tactile and Auditory Marking

It is possible to give the dog information with tactile and auditory cues. This refers to providing a different sound or physical sensation to the dog's paws. If your dog is extremely insecure, tactile and auditory feedback can be valuable.

Pathways can help your dog learn his way between important points in the house. Lay down a path that leads to his food bowl, his safe spot, or the back door. If you have a carpeted floor, lay out plastic or rubber runners. If you have wooden, tile, or linoleum floors, lay down carpet runners. The key is for the pathway to contrast with the existing floor. In this way, the runners will sound and feel different from the surrounding floor.

A variety of plastic and carpet runners are available at carpet stores, home-improvement centers, and some hardware stores. Cut them in half, width-wise, to accommodate small dogs and reduce costs. Tape down the edges of the runners to prevent mishaps.

Teaching the Dog to Negotiate Pathways

Some dogs are hesitant to step on plastic. Place a training treat on the pathway and encourage your dog to eat it. Once your dog is comfortable standing on the runners and receiving food treats, it is time to teach him the benefits of using them.

Lay out one pathway leading to the dog's feeding bowl. When his meal is prepared, hold the bowl under the dog's nose, and lure him along the pathway to his eating area.

When he's finished, use a treat to draw the dog along the pathway leading to the back door. Use a phrase such as, "Do you want to go out?" When you reach the door, reward him with the treat. Repeat this process whenever you think the dog might need to go out.

In the evening when your dog usually relaxes, lure him along the pathway to his bed or safe spot. If you do not have a vocabulary word for this, choose one now. If he wanders off the pathway, reposition the food treat under his nose, and continue leading him along the pathway to his bed. Once there, say your phrase and reward him with the treat. He need not stay in his bed. The goal is to teach him how to find it.

You may also combine scent marking with the use of the pathways by scenting his bed, his bowls, and the back door. Scent part of the pathway approaching the bed with the same scent on the bed, and part of the pathway leading to the door with the same scent on the door, and so on.

Ultimately, even an insecure dog should gain enough confidence to start moving about the house on these pathways. Once these routes are memorized, you will be able to remove the runners. If you do remove them, leave the scent markers for a while longer. Removing both cues simultaneously may cause the dog some difficulty.

If yours is an elderly dog or a SARD dog experiencing rear leg weakness, carpet runners offer an added benefit. When placed over slick floors, they offer a safe and secure place to walk. In these cases, leave the mats down permanently. Maintaining your dog's mobility has positive psychological benefits.

Photo of blind Miniature Schnauzer, "Carlisle,"
courtesy of Angele Fairchild

A variation of using full pathways is to mark troublesome spots with doormats or carpet scraps. Mats can be a warning mark in front of steps and stairs. Mats can indicate the location of the food bowl. One owner reports that when her dog has all four feet on the mat, he knows he's correctly positioned for his dinner bowl. Scrape the bowl along the floor as you set it down. This may also help him locate it.

Additional Auditory Cues

Another method of giving auditory cues is to use a beeper. These are not the paging beepers so many professionals are familiar with, but rather small discs that run on batteries and emit a constant, regular beep. These beepers are designed for human blind patients and are built into a number of devices. (See *Suppliers* list.)

Beepers can serve several functions. They can help a blind dog find an item such as a toy, a water dish, or the doggy door. You can purchase small, battery-powered metronomes at music stores for the same purpose.

Beepers can help a patient avoid obstacles such as a doorjamb, coffee table, or new piece of furniture. Some devices sense motion and allow you to record a message warning the dog to slow down. Be aware, though, if you first teach your dog to avoid the beeping noise, you may have to retrain him if, at a later time, you want him to find a beeping toy.

Going up!

Some beepers can be attached to the dog's collar. They help *you* locate the dog should he become disoriented or lost. These devices are activated with a whistle or remote control.

Give small dogs auditory or tactile cues when you pick them up and move them to a new spot. Teach the dog that he is moving (and no longer on the floor) by using a phrase such as, "Going Up!" Tap the side of the couch or drag his paw on the furniture, as you lift him.

Name the new location to help your dog avoid injury. For example, say, "Tabletop," when you've placed him on the exam table or grooming table. Slide his paw over to feel the table's edge. If he mistakenly believes he is still on the floor, he may unwittingly walk right off the table.

Finally, consider leaving a radio or television playing when you leave the house. If it is the same TV or radio that plays during other times of the day, it will help keep the dog oriented. This is important for blind dogs that may also be experiencing some cognitive (mental) changes.

Furniture Arrangements

Blind-dog owners are commonly told not to change the layout of their furniture. While this advice is helpful in developing the dog's mental map, it does not mean you can never add a piece of furniture or move to a new house. If you make a change in the environment, simply give the dog as many cues possible.

**If you interrupt the old traffic pattern (left) provide cues
that will alert the dog to the new traffic pattern (right).**

For example, if you add a new chair to the room, mark it with a scent on each corner. This provides three-dimensional information to the dog. You can place a beeper on the chair until the dog has memorized its location. Tactile cues may also help the dog. Surround the chair with carpet mats or sheets of newspaper on the floor.

Introduce the dog to the new furniture, on leash. Allow him to walk into the room as he normally would. Give the, "Go Slowly" command as you approach the chair. It is likely that you will have to use gentle pressure on the leash since he has already developed a habit of moving quickly through this area. It may be necessary to repeat this lesson several times.

Sometimes, adapting the furniture can be beneficial. If your small dog becomes tangled and disoriented in the legs of the dining room chairs, wrap them in fabric or clear plastic wrap. Place footstools near the couch or car to increase safety and improve mobility around the house.

The footstool pictured here is actually a small wicker chest covered with a bathmat.

Lightweight steps can be constructed by gluing together thick sheets of styrofoam. This product is available at home improvement stores.

Photo courtesy of *Golden Retrievers in Cyperspace*

Occasionally, moving a piece of furniture *is* the best way to help the dog. If your dog sleeps on your bed, and you are concerned that he will fall off at night, push the bed against one wall. Place the dog on that side. Another option is to place pillows under the covers, around the edge of the bed.

If your dog repeatedly bumps into a particular wall or piece of furniture, protect him from injury until he becomes better oriented. There are a variety of modern packing materials (foams, plastics, etc.) that are available commercially. One such item is pipe insulation. This tubular foam is available at home centers or plumbing-supply stores. Use it as a bumper on the sharp corners of walls and tables. Bubble packing, quilt batting, infant crib bumpers, and double-sided tape are also useful for padding corners.

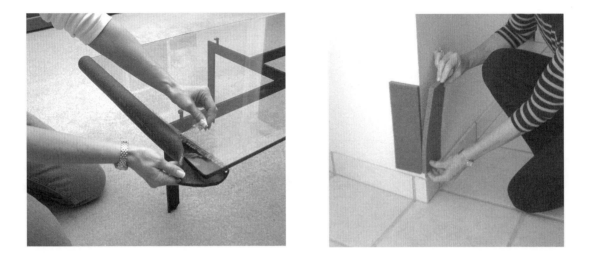

Moving to a New Home

If you relocate, it will be stressful to the dog but you can ease this transition. Mark key locations in your *current* home (the backdoor, his food bowl, and his bed) even if he is well adjusted to his present environment. Mark each item with a different scent.

When you move to the *new* home, his bed and bowls will retain those scents. Mark the new backdoor with the same scent you used in your old home. Another option is to place a beeper or radio at the backdoor, several weeks before you move. Then, place the same device at the backdoor of your new house, after the move.

Introduce your dog to his new home, on leash. Allow the dog to explore only one new room at a time. Block his access to other parts of the house until he is comfortable in the smaller area. This gradual acclimation may take time and effort on your part, but it reduces the dog's stress.

Pack his bed, bowls, and basket of toys in a readily identifiable box so they may be unpacked first. Leave walking paths through the boxes so the dog can begin to learn the layout. Carpet pathways may help during the transition. Crate the dog or confine him to one room when you cannot supervise him.

NOTE: If you must travel away from home, consider what type of arrangements will be made for your dog. For many blind dogs, the best option is to have a dog-sitter come to your house. Kennels will be noisy and confusing. Dog-sitters either stay in your home overnight or come on an hourly basis. If you do not have a relative or friend who is willing to do this, contact your veterinary clinic for a reference. Frequently, members of the veterinary team are available to provide this service.

Physical Assistance

Another method of assisting your dog is by actually restraining him. Some dogs rush headlong into objects. If a dog misjudges the distance necessary to jump off the couch or into the car, injury can result. Restraining him can prevent this. Try to read his body language and anticipate his moves.

If your dog is preparing to jump off of the couch, use the "Wait" command. Restrain him against his chest or collar. A small dog may be picked up at this point. When he wants to jump up onto the couch, give him an auditory cue. Snap your fingers or tap the top of the seat cushion. This will give him an idea of the height necessary to jump. Tell him, "Okay" or "Jump Up." If this is not effective, lift one or both paws to the necessary height and try again.

Restrain the dog before he jumps out of the car or off of the grooming table. Place one hand under his chest. Place the other hand and arm under his loins. Give him the "Okay" to jump down. Help guide him as he does. You need not actually lift him down, but add an element of control to his descent.

With a combination of scent, tactile, and auditory cues, your dog should begin to develop a mental map of your home. Once he does, you may be able to eliminate some of the cues and markers. If your dog becomes confused or stressed, reapply the scent markers and add new tactile or auditory cues. It is not uncommon for dogs to make improvement one day and slip back another day.

NEGOTIATING THE YARD

You can help your blind dog maneuver around the yard, just as you helped him in the house. The main difference being that, outdoors, the dog is at greater risk of injury. Outdoors, there are sharp branches, extremes of weather, and uneven terrain. A few new cues will help your dog avoid injury and still enjoy his time in the yard.

Fencing

Yards and gardens should be fully fenced, especially if your dog is allowed out unattended. Electronic or "invisible" fences are less suitable for blind dogs for several reasons. Blind dogs can become disoriented. In this state, the dog could become so confused that he might actually bear the electrical shock and walk across the fence line. In addition, radio fences do not prevent aggressive dogs from entering your yard.

Metal and wooden fences provide other benefits to blind dogs. Solid fences reflect heat and sound, which provides navigational cues. If your dog has a tendency to run into the fence, add tactile cues on the ground. Lay down a strip of bark chips or gravel several feet wide, along the fence line. Use the *Go Slowly* to teach the dog that these tactile cues indicate the proximity of the fence.

"Bubba," a blind Rottweiler

Limiting Access to Dangerous Areas

Examine your yard from your dog's point of view. Are there holes to fall into or debris to trip your dog? Are there unpruned hedges at the height of your dog's face? A blind dog has little or no blink reflex. Unless he has undergone enucleation (eye removal), this puts him at greater risk of corneal injury.

If your yard is large, consider subdividing it. Section-off a small portion, similar to a dog run, where the dog can relieve himself. This provides a safe area for the dog when you cannot supervise him.

Alternatively, you can limit the dog's access to dangerous areas of the yard. Fence-off landscape ponds or swimming pools. Cover hot tubs. Also fence-off any outdoor staircases until your dog has mastered them.

Decorative landscape fencing is available in wood (small picket fencing), plastic, and wire. Wire covered in green enamel disappears against the landscaping. This is a good compromise between safety and aesthetics.

Placing Scent and Tactile Cues Outdoors

You can scent troublesome spots outdoors: Barbecue stands, patio furniture, and deck poles. Wind and rain will require more frequent reapplications of scent. If the dog continues to bump into certain items, pad them until the dog has developed a better mental map. The extra effort is worth avoiding injury.

Some dogs have difficulty finding their way when called in from the yard. These dogs are disoriented, not disobedient. They are trying to come in the house, but don't know which way to turn. The problem is worse during stormy, windy weather when it's difficult to hear and track scents.

If possible, lay a pathway from the center of the yard, toward the door. Use gravel, fresh bark chips (which also provide a scent cue), brick, or stone. These materials will sound and feel different from the grass. Sprinkle bark chips or straw pathways over fresh snow.

Provide your dog with additional landmarks. This is especially helpful in wide-open, level yards that provide few orientation cues. Hang wind chimes or a large bell near the back door. Plant fragrant flowers or herbs along pathways. Rosemary remains fragrant until it is covered by deep snow.

Introduce your dog to outdoor pathways in the same way you did indoors. Ring the chimes or bell. Walk out onto the pathway and call your dog toward you with your continuous sound. Lure him along the path. When you reach the back door, reward him. In time, the dog will develop a mental map of how to follow the path and find the door.

The concept of following the path is especially valuable if your dog has free access to the yard via a doggy-door. With free access, the dog might become disoriented, unbeknownst to you. An understanding of pathways can help minimize this problem.

If your dog continues to have trouble, it may be best to accompany the dog outdoors. One owner attaches a long line to her dog. In this way she can reel in the line and guide him back to the house.

Photo of blind Doberman Pinscher, "Ralph," courtesy of Deborah Wiebe

Here, patio stones have been placed at the bottom of the porch/deck steps, while pots of scented flowers (left) have been placed at the top. Yet other flowers indicate the location of the fence line (background).

Doggy-Doors

If your house is not equipped with a doggy-door, consider installing one now. These doors can be beneficial for older, blind dogs that may be unable to wait as long as they once did to relieve themselves. If you already have a doggy door, remind your dog how to use it.

This plush bathmat provides a visual and tactile contrast to the hard vinyl flooring.

Teaching the Dog to Negotiate the Doggy-Door

Sometimes a dog must step up several inches in order to clear the threshold. Have the dog eat a treat from the door's threshold or tap the threshold with your hand. Food and auditory cues provide information as to how high he must step. You can even lift up his paw and place it on the threshold.

Hold the flap up with one hand, and lure the dog through the door with a training treat. If he is hesitant, use the treat-dropped-on-newspaper technique described previously. Drop a food treat on the other side of the door. As he steps through the door, use a verbal cue such as "Through" or "Go Out."

Once the dog is comfortable at this stage, lower the flap onto his back as he passes through the door. Continue lowering the flap, until he must push past it. Mark both sides of the doggy-door with scents with tactile cues (mats indoors, gravel outdoors, etc.)

Dealing With Incontinence — Accidents in the House

There is some speculation that a newly blind dog may mark his territory to provide navigational cues. If you suspect this to be true, review the sections on scent marking and tactile cues. Dominant dogs may mark when a new dog is added to the household. Bladder infections can cause incontinence, as can a number of systemic diseases and medications. Do *not* withhold water from dogs with SARD, Cushing's disease, diabetes mellitus, and those taking steroids, or anti-seizure medications.

There are several ways to minimize accidents in the house. Take notice of your dog's schedule, his water intake, and his body language. Some dogs are better than others about asking to go out. They make eye contact, wander near the door, or whine. Other dogs never ask. The owners of these dogs must pay attention to the clock (when was the last time the dog went out?) and encourage the dog to go again.

Dogs typically need to urinate after play and napping. Dogs frequently need to defecate after a meal and when they go for a walk. Dogs differ in their schedules and in frequency. If you are trying to housebreak a puppy or a rescue dog, please see the discussion of crate training in Chapter 15, *Dogs Blind From Birth*.

Have a specific word or phrase for elimination. Some owners say, "Do Your Business" or "Go Potty." Once he is done, tell him, "Good Business" or "Good Potty," and reward him with a food treat.

If your dog does have an accident, do not carry-on about it. In many cases, these are not lapses in house training but rather, uncontrollable accidents. Calmly help the dog out the door and say the phrase for him to eliminate, reminding him that the outdoors is the appropriate place for this.

Yelling and spanking him will only make the dog more nervous about eliminating. A nervous dog is even less likely to ask to go out. You can clean up the accident while the dog is outdoors.

Cleaning Up

Deodorizing the spot reduces the chance of another accident in the same area. One of the oldest and best remedies is white vinegar. For urine accidents on carpet, repeatedly blot up the area. Lean your weight against small piles of towels, until no more appears to soak up.

Photo of blind Australian Terrier, "Mindy," courtesy of Claudette Trimblay

Saturate the area with a mixture of half water, half vinegar, and cover it with a towel so that dirt is not tracked through it. If it smells of anything other than the faint fragrance of vinegar after a day or two, repeat the process. Vinegar can also be used to deodorize the area after a solid waste accident.

Other Solutions to Incontinence

If you believe your dog is capable of getting outdoors but continues to have accidents in the house, make some concessions for him. Consider purchasing house-breaking pads. These are a combination of a paper towel and a plastic backing. They are often scented to attract puppies to eliminate on them. Some owners buy incontinence pads designed for bed-ridden, hospital patients. These are larger than puppy pads. If the dog has repeatedly had accidents in the same place, put the pads there.

If there is a place in the house, garage, laundry room, etc., where you would be willing to let the dog relieve himself, put the pads there. Since most dogs do not like eliminating in the house once they have been housebroken, you may have to retrain him.

Lead him to the spot at a time when he normally relieves himself. Give your command and tap the paper pads. Reward him if he eliminates.

The owner of one large, geriatric dog is unable to arrive home from work before her dog needs to relieve himself. She set up a small, rigid, plastic swimming pool (the type that is about eight to ten inches high), lined it with newspapers, and placed it in her basement.

One owner purchased a baby monitor. With one monitor by the dog's bed, and one by the backdoor, she is able to hear when the dog needs to go out. You can also purchase the type of rigid, plastic carpet protector that fits underneath rolling desk chairs. It will allow you to hear the dog's toenails if he gets out of bed during the night. The plastic also protects the carpeting below. Plastic drop clothes and plastic-lined mattress pads serve the same purpose. Mattress pads can also be used to cover favorite furniture.

Some people move the dog's sleeping quarters into a tiled or vinyl-floored bathroom. And there are certain dog beds available that allow urine to pass through webbed bedding to a pan below. (See *Suppliers* section.)

You can purchase or construct doggy diapers for incontinent pets. For male dogs, purchase a regular diaper for human infants and several elastic dress clips (the type used to gather the fabric on the back of a dress). These are sold in fabric and fashion-accessory stores. You can find similar elasticized clips in the bed and linen department. Apply the diaper like a cummerbund. Line the diaper with feminine sanitary pads for additional absorbency. Diapers for female dogs are available commercially.

A number of dog owners report that dietary changes reduce incontinence. Eliminating grain from the dog's diet often improves bladder control. This may be linked to the cycle of inflammation, cortisol production, and muscle weakness that grain protein is believed to induce.

While some of these measures may seem extravagant, they can benefit both dog and owner. Creating a situation where the dog can continue to be a clean and tidy pet improves the quality of his life, and probably yours, as well.

NEGOTIATING THE COMMUNITY

By now, you and your dog have had practice with new exercises and vocabulary. Now, you may be ready to negotiate areas more complex than just the house and yard. This could mean taking a walk to the mailbox, around the neighborhood, or a trip to the veterinarian's office. In some situations your dog will be able to build a mental map of the area. In others, he will benefit from your guidance.

Why Take Your Blind Dog Out in Public

Some dogs are nervous and unhappy in public. Sometimes this is related to the blindness. Other times it is related to poor socialization during puppyhood or abuse. These dogs are sometimes happiest at home.

Most dogs, however, are delighted to get out of the house. Make an effort to take your blind dog out. While it may require a little more effort on your part, it is a treat for the dog. As social creatures, they crave contact with others. Public outings stimulate the dog's mind and exercise his body. Providing the dog with skills to accompany you in public can minimize depression and reduce dependent behaviors.

You may notice that various weather and lighting conditions help or hinder your dog. Dogs with partial cataracts or dilated pupils may falter in their first few steps outdoors. They may require a few moments to adjust to the bright light. The owners of some SARD dogs believe that their dogs function best in the evening.

"Carlisle," a blind Miniature Schnauzer

Human patients with low vision report that bright, cloudy days present difficult conditions. On these days, light waves bounce off the clouds and back to earth, creating glare. If this continues to be a problem, adjust your schedule or provide your dog some shade. Sun-visor hats for dogs are available commercially. (See *Suppliers* section.)

Low light and windy conditions can also cause problems. Dogs in the early stages of PRA will have more trouble in low light. Windy conditions reduce a dog's ability to hear you or smell you, should you become separated.

Providing Auditory Feedback to Your Dog

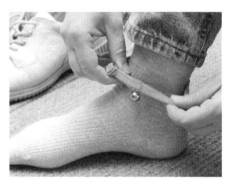

Since your dog cannot see you when you take a walk, assist him with auditory cues. If you are uncomfortable singing, whistling, or talking to your dog, try some other options. Wear a cat collar-bell on your ankle or hip. During the Christmas season, it is possible to purchase shoelaces or socks with bells on them.

If that is still uncomfortable for you, wear a pair of shoes that squeak or carry a transistor radio on your walk. Try one of the beepers or battery-powered metronomes previously mentioned. The knowledge that you are close will help build your dog's confidence.

If you own a dog that is shy of loud noises, it is especially important for you to bring training treats with you in public. When your dog exhibits signs of fear, don't pick him up or pet him. Feed him, instead. He will focus on the food and learn to ignore the noise.

Helping Your Dog Build a Mental Map of the Neighborhood

Your dog will develop a mental map of your house after many repeated trips through the rooms. Likewise, your dog will build a mental map of your neighborhood or park if you take him on the same route every time. While this may seem boring to you, it can be enjoyable for the dog.

There are two advantages to walking a routine course through your neighborhood. First, as your dog develops a mental map, he will gain confidence. You will find less need to guide him, making the walk less work and more relaxing for you. Second, if your dog ever got loose, odds are that he might take the same route. This would improve your chances of finding him.

Meeting New People

Dogs respond differently when meeting strangers. Some dogs crave this social contact; some dogs shy from it. They may cringe, growl, or bite. Since your dog may find himself in contact with the veterinarian, the groomer, or perhaps an unsuspecting child, it is important that he accept physical contact from others.

Teaching Your Dog to Accept a Stranger's Touch

Help a dog overcome his dislike of strangers with food rewards. Be sure to have training treats with you when you are out in public. Choose a phrase to alert the dog that someone is about to touch him. Tell people who want to handle your dog to use this same phrase. For example, tell the veterinary staff, "Before you examine him, say, 'Hands on.'"

When you give strangers permission to pet your dog, have the person hold out his hand to be sniffed. You (his leader) may then give the dog a treat. The person may then slowly pet the dog, while you feed him another treat. If you are consistent, he should eventually learn to tolerate this contact.

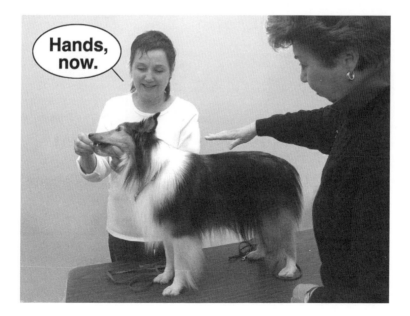

Using Humor to Deal with Blindness

Human blind patients sometimes find it tiresome to repeatedly discuss their condition with strangers. They share stories of how to use humor. One human patient tells of two message buttons she wears pinned to her coat. One reads "Speak up, I'm blind." The other reads, "I may look good, but I don't see well."

Blind-dog owners also find help in the use of humor. One owner "assisted" her dog in writing about his blindness. Together, they came up with this:

<u>Top 10 Reasons It's Good to be Blind</u>

#10 – It makes my human pick up her junk.

#9 – My human has stopped the annoying habit of rearranging the furniture.

#8 – I can "milk" visitors for extra petting and treats.

#7 – My human gets out of *my* way, instead of insisting I get out of hers.

#6 – I will never have to see those horrible kites anymore.
       (Beware, fellow dogs…kites are alive and out to get us!)

#5 – No more eerie light from fires and candle . . . (also out to get us).

#4 – I don't have to pay attention to silly hand signals anymore.

#3 – It doesn't matter what I break. My human just gets out the broom.

#2 – It makes my human do the silliest things, like using her expensive perfume on the staircase.

And, the number one reason it is good to be blind: I can drive my human crazy by staring out the window. She can't figure out what I'm looking at!

(Reprinted with permission from the author who wishes to remain anonymous.)

Meeting New Dogs

Don't be afraid to explain your dog's blindness to other people. It will help them control their dogs as needed. All blind dogs are at a distinct disadvantage when meeting new dogs. Specifically, they are "body-language mutes" — unable to see, read, and interpret body language. (Review page 49 for details.) Consequently, blind dogs don't always respond in ways the other dog expects.

Without these cues, your dog may feel threatened when meeting other dogs. The *other* dog may act inappropriately in these situations. A classic example is when a blind dog meets a dominant dog. The alpha dog displays dominant behaviors. The blind dog does not react. The dominant dog becomes increasingly aggressive. If this occurs within your own pack, strongly discourage the aggressive behavior.

Decide which dogs you will allow your own dog to meet and greet. Be aware that dogs on leash may feel confined (threatened) and behave more protectively of you, their owner.

As another dog approaches, call out to his owner, "Is your dog friendly? My dog is blind." Repeat yourself, until you receive a reply. If your dog is small, and you fear for his safety, you may lift him up to remove him from danger. Otherwise, simply turn and briskly walk in the opposite direction from the approaching dog. Use the "Forward" command to remove your dog from a potentially dangerous situation.

It is strongly suspected that dogs take their behavioral cues from you, their leader. If you are friendly and relaxed when meeting another dog, it is likely the dogs will be, too. If your voice is pleasant and relaxed when you say, "What a lovely dog you have," you are providing your dog with similar information.

Teaching Your Dog That Another Dog Approaches

If you frequently meet other dogs while you are out, teach your dog a phrase to indicate that another dog is approaching. Start by enlisting the help of a friend who owns a social dog. Have both dogs on leash.

Ask your friend to take his dog about 10 feet away from yours. Give your dog a cue such as, "Here comes a dog!" Instruct your friend to walk toward you. Allow the dogs to greet each other for a moment, and then repeat.

If your dog is uncomfortable meeting other dogs, provide positive reinforcement with this exercise. After the verbal cue, give your dog a food treat. Be cautious about feeding your dog when the other dog gets close, however. Dogs can become territorial and aggressive over food.

Riding in the Car

Many of the cues used in the house will transfer to use in the car. Mark the threshold (the height the dog must jump up) with scent or contrasting tape. Mark the dog's crate or bed with scents or mats. Use auditory cues to indicate where you want him to move. Tap, snap your fingers, or jingle your car keys. Give him a treat when he follows the sound. Consider using ramps for large dogs.

Avoid the practice of allowing your dog to hang his head out of the car window at high speeds. With little or no blink relex, blind dogs are at greater risk of injury from flying debris. There is also some question as to whether high wind pressure raises intraocular pressure.

Use the *Wait* exercise if you must move something out of the way before the dog can jump in. Use it when you wish to lift his paw to the height of the door threshold.

Also, use the command before you let the dog out of the car. This allows you time to place your hand under the dog's chest and guide him to the ground.

If your dog is not crated, consider purchasing a seat belt harness designed for dogs. If your dog stands while the car is in motion, he might benefit from a few additional cues from you. One owner says, "Hang on!" before she turns a corner. This helps the dog brace himself and maintain balance during the ride.

Traveling and Camping With Your Blind Dog

If you plan an extended trip with your dog, refresh his training before you go. Consider purchasing an exercise pen (ex-pen) — a portable, wire pen that provides a dog with a safe area. Introduce him to the ex-pen in short periods in your home. Take it with you when you travel. If you take your dog camping, set up the ex-pen in the same place each time. For example, one owner sets up the pen immediately outside the camper door, on the left.

Photo of Golden Retrievers, "Sebaca" and "Sandy" (blind)
courtesy of Bev Barna

Before you travel, scent-mark your back door, his safe spot, and his water/food bowls with different scents. When you visit family, friends, or a hotel, use the same scents to mark these areas. This may help locate important areas in new environments.

Geriatric dogs are less capable of handling extremes of weather. SARD and diabetic dogs can have difficulty tolerating heat. It may be best to minimize travel for these dogs. Arrange for groomers and veterinarians to come to you if your dog does not travel well. This may be an expense, but it is certainly much less stressful for some dogs.

NOTE: Groomers should be instructed not to clip the whiskers of blind dogs. These whiskers are sensory organs and may help the dog avoid obstacles.

PLAYTIME

In the wild, play teaches puppies the skills necessary for hunting and socializing with other pack members. Play keeps domesticated dogs physically fit and entertained. It can help reduce stress and relieve boredom. There are a number of toys and games that are especially appropriate for blind dogs. See the *Suppliers* section to learn more about the toys discussed in this chapter.

Why Play With Your Dog

Playtime is especially valuable for young or high-energy dogs that have gone blind. These dogs may no longer receive the same level of exercise they once did. They may store up enormous amounts of energy. If this energy isn't suitably directed, it may be expressed as undesirable behaviors such as destructive digging, chewing, and excessive barking. Mental activity — playing games in which the dog must think — can provide many of the same benefits that physical exercise produces.

How to Play With a Blind Dog

The key to playing with a blind dog is to capitalize on his senses of hearing and smell, while minimizing the risk of injury. Dogs take great pleasure in games revolving around their natural prey and hunting instincts. Your dog may enjoy the game best when he is allowed to find and capture his prey (the toy). Play with your dog in open areas that are free of obstacles.

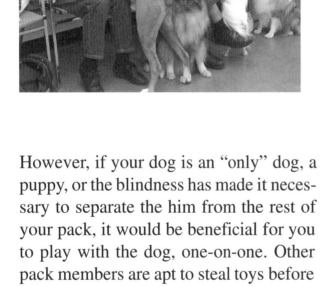

Dogs, like people, are social creatures. As pack animals, dogs generally enjoy the company of other dogs.

However, if your dog is an "only" dog, a puppy, or the blindness has made it necessary to separate the him from the rest of your pack, it would be beneficial for you to play with the dog, one-on-one. Other pack members are apt to steal toys before the blind dog can find them. This is also true of games involving food.

Slowly introduce your dog to new games. If a dog doesn't understand the game, he may become frustrated, insecure, or depressed. Unless your dog has aggressive tendencies, ensure that he can win the game much of the time.

If your dog does not seem playful, be patient. He may still be adjusting to the blindness or he may be too stressed to enjoy playing. He may also be experiencing systemic (body-wide) symptoms from other conditions. For example, lethargy is a common symptom of SARD, Cushing's disease, and uncontrolled diabetes.

If time passes and he is still disinterested in play, experiment with new toys. Dogs, like children, are individuals. A toy cherished by one pet may hold no interest for another, and vice versa. Try different toys to see what your dog likes. Keep his toys in one spot so he can always find them when he wants to play.

NOTE: Take great care when selecting toys for your dog. If a toy is not specifically designed for chewing, it may break into smaller pieces, causing your dog gastric upset or injury. If you have questions regarding the safety of a toy, please consult the salesperson before making the purchase.

Monitor your dog each time you give him a new toy. Note whether it holds up to chewing and other vigorous activity. Also note whether it is so small that your dog could conceivably swallow it whole. Some of the toys mentioned in the following sections are *not* designed for unsupervised play. These are toys for the dog to play with only in your company.

One owner explains that, initially, her dog was frightened by his new toy. In fact, when she brought out the toy, the dog left the room! Some blind dogs are fearful of new things, even toys. Spend a few minutes introducing the toy to your dog. Use food treats to help alleviate his fears.

In addition, it may help your dog if he realizes that *you* enjoy playing with a toy. Talk excitedly to your dog about the new toy. Handle it and play with it yourself, to peak his interest.

Some dogs literally do not know how to play. This may be due to abuse or neglect they have suffered. Sometimes progress is slow, but these dogs eventually get the idea and copy your behaviors.

Games of Sound

Photo of blind Chesapeake Bay Retriever,
"Ceska" courtesy of Maggie Buck

Many dogs delight in games of retrieving. Such games revolve around the dog's prey drive. One owner shares a remarkable example of just what dogs can learn. When her dog loses track of the ball, she plays the "hot" and "cold" word game with the dog. He understands that "cold" means he is not at the ball and tries a different place. He knows that "warm" means he is getting closer and "hot" means he is just about on top of it. Other owners use "right" and "left" to help the dog. You can also whistle as the dog gets closer to the toy.

Balls and Flying Discs

Since blind dogs cannot see where the ball is thrown, choose toys that make noise for extended periods of time. Purchase a rubber ball with a bell inside. It is also possible to find balls made for toddlers, which have small music boxes inside. Since these balls are not specifically designed for dog play, it is important to supervise your dog with these.

If you want something more high tech, investigate toys made for blind humans. Balls are available in cloth, foam, plastic, and leather. Some are equipped with bells inside, others with beepers. Flying discs that beep — similar to a Frisbee® toy — are also appropriate. Some whistle as they travel through the air. Look for these at childrens' toy stores. It is also possible to purchase beepers or metronomes individually and tuck them into your own toys.

One way to do this is to purchase a toy called the Hol-ee Roller. This is a rubber ball with an open, web-shaped design. (If your dog enjoys water retrieves, purchase the Hol-ee *Floater* version of this toy. It has an air-filled, plastic toy in the center of the rubber ball, which keeps it afloat.) Insert a small metronome into a bag of bubble wrapping, a wide-

mouth, plastic jar, or waterproof cell-phone case. Then insert both into the ball. (See *Suppliers* section.)

Photos of blind Labrador Retriever,
"Maggie" and her toy, courtesy of
Catherine Jamieson

To introduce the ball or disc to your dog, pretend it is the most wonderful toy in the world. This is especially important if you are using a toy with a beeper and have previously trained your dog to *avoid* the beeping sound.

Once you have played with the dog and the ball at close range, slowly roll it a short distance away from you. Verbally encourage your dog to get it. If your dog fails to follow it, call him over to where it is, pick it up and play with it at close range again.

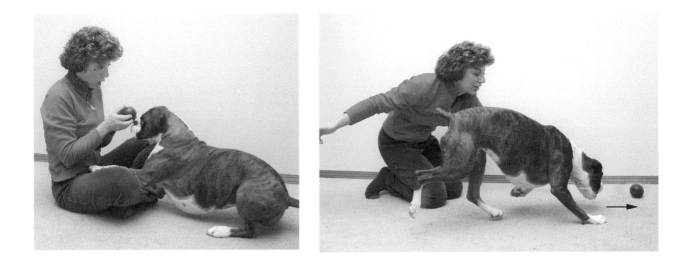

After a moment, try rolling it away again. If you are using a ball with a bell, it must roll slowly enough so the bell is still sounding when the dog reaches it. Your dog will likely use a combination of hearing and scenting abilities to find the ball.

Some owners have experimented with balls and other toys originally designed for cats. Some contain small motors that make noise that the dog can follow. Be careful with these if your dog is a vigorous chewer. These balls are manufactured of hard plastic that could break into shards. Radio-controlled mice and remote controlled racecars may also be suitable for some blind dogs.

Fuzzy Animal Toys

Presently, numerous plush, fuzzy toys are available which emit long sounds. These toys go by the name *Look Who's Talking*® or *Tug-and-Talk*® and include a racecar, train, walrus, whale, tiger, and duck, to name just a few. They make recorded noises specific to the toy. For example, the train engine makes a "chug-a-chug-a" sound, followed by a steam whistle. It is surprising and delightful technology.

It is also possible to find this technology in childrens' toy stores. These plush toys represent popular story characters. Some even allow you to record a short message on a built-in recorder. If you buy these for your dog, examine them first for safety. Since they are not specifically designed for dogs, they may have small, plastic parts that can be chewed off and swallowed.

Purchase balls and toys that talk or giggle.

These toys have two advantages over balls. They may be more pleasing to your dog because of their tactile (fuzzy) nature. And they can be thrown a greater distance while still making noise. This helps the dog to find them once they've landed. In this way, the dog can expend more energy.

If your dog is an aggressive chewer and rips apart his toys, there is another option. Purchase one of the remote-controlled beepers designed for blind humans. Use the stuffing from an old toy, pillow, or quilt batting, and tuck both the stuffing and the beeper into a fake-sheepskin, car-washing mitten. Tuck the wristband inside and sew it shut with heavy thread. These mitts are extremely durable.

Tag and Monkey-in-the-Middle

Involve your whole family in dog play. To play monkey-in-the-middle, have two or more people stand several feet apart from each other. Provide each human with a supply of training treats. One person begins by calling the dog, much like you have practiced in the *Recall* exercise. Remember to use a continuous sound, whistle, clicker, or squeaky toy.

As soon as the dog has received his treat, another person calls the dog. When the dog reaches the second person, another food treat is earned. Eventually, family members can spread out until the dog is running back and forth to receive his treats.

Playing this game with multiple dogs has pros and cons. On one hand, it is possible for the blind dog to become trampled or disoriented by other dogs bumping into him. On the other hand, the blind dog may catch on more quickly and enjoy the vigor of having companions. It may be especially helpful if the other dogs are wearing bells. Evaluate your particular pack.

The game of tag is a mild variation of monkey-in-the-middle. Once the dog reaches you and receives his treat, run off a few feet and call your dog again. Carry a bell or beeper. If you own multiple dogs, you may notice them playing this game by themselves.

Games of Scent

Many of today's breeds (especially the hounds) were developed specifically for their ability to follow an animal's scent. It is an important survival skill in terms of hunting. Even breeds that were *not* bred to track have an amazing ability to scent — one that far surpasses ours.

Photo of blind Chesapeake Bay Retriever, "Ceska" courtesy of Maggie Buck

Scenting games do require some thought and energy on your part, but they can be worked into your daily schedule with a little planning. If you and your dog enjoy these scent games, consider pursuing more organized tracking activities.

Tracking clubs are located all around the United States and tracking is a sport recognized by the American Kennel Club (AKC). While blind dogs are not permitted to compete for AKC tracking titles, you might enjoy visiting a club event to learn more about these activities.

Follow-the-Food Trail

This is the first, and easiest, scenting game to play with your dog. The object is for the dog to follow a food trail through the house or yard, until he locates and captures a toy. Most dogs take utter delight in this type of activity. Prepare the game while the dog is in another room or outdoors.

Since your dog is already familiar with following a sound to find a reward, he should come to understand this game as well. In this game, he will follow a trail of food to find the toy. This game does not require a noisy toy.

When numerous scents are present, it may be confusing for the dog, so choose a room that has *not* been heavily scented with fragrant oils or perfumes. It is also helpful if you choose a room that does not receive much foot traffic. A spare bedroom or formal dining room is a good choice.

Move the furniture so that there is an open area in which to play. (You may certainly play these games outdoors, but initially, it may be more difficult for the dog to learn the game amidst wildlife tracks.)

Place a trail of food treats starting from the entrance of the room, leading several feet into the room. Start by placing each treat about six inches apart. As the dog advances in skill, space the treats further apart. At the end of the trail, place the dog's favorite toy.

To start the game, bring the dog into the room. You may need to restrain him slightly, so that he doesn't walk through the line of treats. Alert him to the first treat by tapping the floor. You may need to lift it up to his nose and then replace it on the floor. As he moves along the trail, use a phrase such as "get the cookie" or "find it." Tap the floor near the next treat and use your phrase.

Your dog may scout around, rather than directly following the path of treats. Dogs hunt around to ensure that they have not missed any food. Continue tapping the floor from one treat to the next.

When your dog reaches the toy, be terribly excited for him! Dogs love to feel as though they have completed their job. It is also a way to tell the dog that the game has ended and he has achieved the goal.

With time, lengthen the trail and the distance between the treats. You can lay the trail from room to room. You can hide the toy behind obstacles once your dog is more skilled. This eventually becomes a game of hide-and-seek.

If you play this game often, remember to decrease your dog's dinner rations. Also, periodically change locations where you play. In this way, you will allow the scent of a previous trail to fade away, reducing confusion for the dog.

Tracking the Toy

In this scent game, the object is to drag a toy or other scented item, creating a scent path for the dog to follow. As with the previous game, this too, becomes a game of hide-and-seek. You might find it helpful to purchase a new toy with a strong scent (new rubber toys, smoked bones, or scented tennis balls).

There are a variety of hard, rubber toys available with handy crevices and niches in which to tuck food. Examples include the Kong toys (Cool Kong even comes with a rope attached), Yapples (round balls with holes for peanut butter, cream cheese, or liverwurst), and Goodie Gripper® Ships (shaped, as the name implies, like spaceships). You may even tie a string around a dog biscuit for this game.

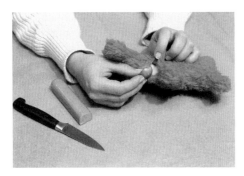

If you don't wish to use food, purchase an animal pelt, such as rabbit skin or sheepskin. Allow your dog to play with the pelt only under supervision. Some dogs will chew and swallow these pelts, causing themselves gastric upset.

It is not necessary to purchase a new toy for this game, however. If you wish to use an older toy, try scenting it with something exciting. Tuck a piece of hot dog or cheese into a crevice or rub your hands on the toy after you have handled a piece of hot dog or cheese.

When a treat is tucked into a toy, the food need not actually come into direct contact with carpeting, because dogs scent in two ways. Dogs either track scent molecules along the ground or they air scent. In this case, they will follow the scent molecules left in the air.

Lay out the game while the dog is in another part of the house or waiting outdoors. Tie a string around the toy or pelt. Starting at the entrance, drag it several feet into the room. (Again, a room that receives less traffic is best for scent games.)

Remember to restrain the dog when you first allow him into the room, so that he doesn't walk through the set-up. Tap the ground where you started the trail and ask, "Where's your toy?" or "Find it!" Continue tapping the ground along the trail until he reaches the toy or pelt.

As with the food trail game, you can play track-the-toy through many rooms of the house, in the yard, or even through the park or countryside. Just remember where you laid the path, so that if your dog becomes confused, you can lead him back to it.

If you do pursue scent games outdoors, keep in mind that the scent molecules are affected by the weather. Cool, humid conditions (but not rain), make scenting easier. These conditions hold down the scent molecules closer to the earth. Dry, windy, and hot weather makes scenting more difficult, as scent molecules rise from the earth under these conditions.

Additional Toys for Scenting

There are a few more toys presently available that are good for blind dogs. Some of these toys deliver food treats to the dog when rolled across the floor. One is called the Buster Cube, another is the Training Treat Ball, and a third is called Havaball.

The Buster Cube is a plastic cube with a cylindrical opening on one side. Treats are poured into the cylinder and then roll into various compartments of the cube. The dog rolls the cube along the ground, trying to get the treats, and tracking those that have tumbled out. Remember to adjust your dog's meal rations if you play this game often.

Both the Treat Ball and the Havaball have a simpler design, but with the same philosophy. One model, the Talk-to-Me Treat Ball, permits you to record a message to your dog. It is inadvisable to leave a dog unattended with toys made of hard plastic. Dogs have been known to crush the toys into sharp shards. The Havaball is made of rubber and may be better suited to unsupervised play.

Toys that dispense food entertain the dog, including Havaballs (right) and the Buster Cube (center). Even old balls with holes or plastic soda bottles will work.

If these toys are unavailable to you, improvise with other things. Place dog biscuits in lengths of old fabric or blanket and tie them into a series of knots. Gnawing at the knots will provide a similar challenge to the dog. Scent old tennis balls by placing them in a bag with a few peanuts and roll them (instead of throwing them) for the dog.

In general, it is advisable to have chew toys and bones available to the dog. Chewing is an instinctual and beneficial activity among dogs. Blind dogs are sometimes less active than sighted dogs, yet still require entertainment. Chew toys and bones provide an absorbing activity and appropriate energy release. If you have several dogs, purchase enough chew toys for all.

Water Play

Some blind-dog owners do allow their dogs to swim and enjoy water retrieves. These owners also report that the dogs are kept on long lines or under close scrutiny at all times. Doggy life preservers (also called personal floatation devices or PFDs) are available for dogs weighing 20 to 120 pounds.

Photo of blind Golden Retriever, "Kate"
courtesy of Garrie Stevens

One owner places a beeper inside a retrieving "bumper" or "dummy" (the type used to train hunting dogs). The dog follows the sound to retrieve it. If your dog has partial vision, purchase balls that float above the water level. Some large balls have ropes attached to facilitate retrieving.

Photo of Labrador Retrievers, "Maggie" (blind)
and "Pilot" courtesy of Catherine Jamieson

It is also possible to purchase bottled musk oils of a various game animals including duck, quail, deer, and rabbit. These scents are typically used to help hunting dogs with their retrieval work, but they may also work nicely for your dog, too.

Group Dog Play

It is wise, initially, for you to monitor any type of group play. This refers to multiple-dog households when a pack member first goes blind, as well as when your dog plays with dogs you don't own. One of two things can happen. The pack members might turn against the blind dog or they will try to help him.

One owner relates a fascinating story of how his dogs learned to play tag. The blind dog could not see the other dogs that were running toward, and then *into*, him. The blind dog became disoriented and turned around, until he was facing entirely away from the group.

One of the sighted dogs barked at the blind dog, which promptly turned him back around. As the owner explains, "It was as though the other dog was saying, 'Hey, over here, Silly!'" The sighted dog moved ninety degrees to one side and barked again. The blind dog turned ninety degrees. The sighted dog moved and barked again. The blind dog turned once more. And so it was that this group of dogs learned some new rules about how to include their blind companion in play.

Another owner reports that her blind dog's excessive barking can upset dogs that aren't used to it. If you find the same to be true, become involved in the play yourself. Literally tell these dogs that everything is "Okay." Dogs will take their cues from their humans. If the pack realizes that you, the leader, are at ease with the barking, they should become more comfortable, too.

Another reason to monitor group play involves safety. If the dogs become particularly boisterous, there is a chance that the blind dog could be injured. Blind dogs have little, if any, blink reflex. Corneal injuries are exceedingly painful and can heal slowly, especially in the presence of other conditions such as diabetes, Cushing's disease, and SARD. Perforating injuries may lead to enucleation (surgical removal of the eye).

It may be necessary to teach all of the dogs in your house terms such as, "Easy." While most of us enjoy watching our dogs play, it is your position as the pack leader to monitor and direct group activity when it becomes a safety hazard.

Companions for "Only" Dogs

If your dog is a sub-alpha and an "only" dog, consider arranging playtime with other social dogs. This is especially important if your blind dog is a puppy. If your dog has an alpha (dominant, aggressive) personality, he may not be interested in canine companionship.

Invite other friendly dogs to play in your house or yard. It is also possible for the two of you to visit the homes of friendly dogs. Bear in mind that this might prove a little more difficult for your dog since he may not have a good mental map of the environment. Watch your dog's body language for cues as to whether he is enjoying himself. If he does not seem comfortable, return to playing one on one.

Keep safe toys in one spot where the dog can find them.

WHITE CANES AND OTHER DEVICES

Blind people use white canes to maintain mobility. A number of clever dog owners have constructed similar devices to help their dogs. (See the *Suppliers* section. Several of these items are available commercially.) Some devices alert dogs to obstacles, some may help prevent injuries, and others attempt to do both. Dogs learn to tap, bounce, or feel their way with these devices.

Not all devices are well suited to all dogs, however. Some dogs are intolerant of having clothing or any other sort of an apparatus strapped to them. If your dog is one of these, focus instead on training and scent cues.

Photo courtesy of Bev Barna

Eye and Head Protection

Since blind dogs have poor, if any, blink reflex, goggles may help them avoid injury. Introduce your dog to the goggles while he is on carpet or grass. If your dog tries to scrape off the goggles on concrete or rocks, he can permanently scratch the lenses.

Baseball-style caps or sun-visors are also available for dogs. They strap underneath the dog's chin, around his ears, and attach to his collar. If the brim is sufficiently long, caps may alert the dog to obstacles before facial contact is made.

Collar Canes

Several white-cane equivalents or "feelers" have been devised for dog collars. In the first example, the feelers (plastic cable straps/loops) protrude from the collar like the rays of the sun. Purchase plastic tie-down loops at a hardware or home improvement store. Attach them at frequent intervals along the dog's collar. Position them at a slightly forward angle. This design is effective in locating obstacles mainly to the dog's side.

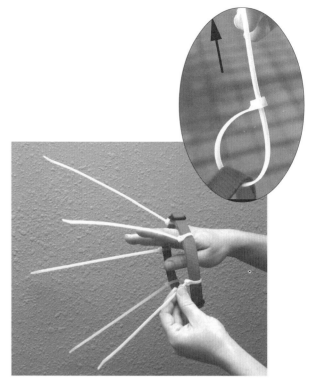

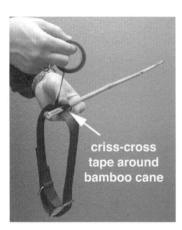

criss-cross tape around bamboo cane

In order to help the dog identify obstacles directly in his path, a different design is required. If a dog's collar rides high on his neck, some owners affix a thin bamboo cane (available at the craft or garden store) to the top of the collar.

One owner developed a more substantial design in which feelers are mounted on each side of the collar. This device is sturdy, but is still comfortable when the dog lies down.

To build this device for your own dog, purchase the following:
- A heavy leather collar
- Two plastic tie-down straps: 1/4 inch x 15 inches
- A 12-inch length of rubber fuel line: 3/8 inch, available at auto parts supply stores
- Two smooth rivets or two bolts and screws: 3/16 inch x 1 inch; plus four washers

To construct this collar cane, first buckle the collar on your dog and rotate the buckle until it is under the dog's neck. Mark each side of the collar at the mid-point. This is where the canes will attach, balancing the collar and keeping it upright. Remove the collar and drill or punch a hole at each point. The hole should be slightly smaller than the bolt or rivet.

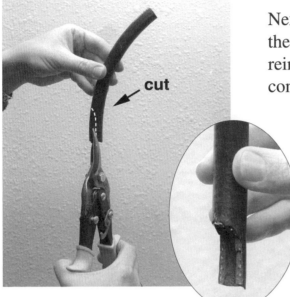

Next, cut the fuel line into two, 6-inch pieces. (Cut the pieces shorter for small dogs.) This tubing will reinforce the plastic feelers. This type of fuel line comes on a roll, so it is usually slightly curved.

Lay out the tubes so they curve toward each other. This will discourage the plastic canes from splaying apart. Bevel one end of each tube by cutting off a slight angle. Cut the *outer* curve of the tube. This bevel will allow you to mount the tubing close to the collar. Drill or punch a hole through the inner curve of the beveled end.

Pass one of the plastic tie-down straps (canes) through a piece of rubber tubing. Line up the hole in the rubber tubing with the hole in the plastic cane. Slide the collar between the beveled tubing and the plastic cane so that the rubber tubing is on the inside of the collar. Be sure that the pieces of rubber tubing will curve toward each other when the collar is buckled.

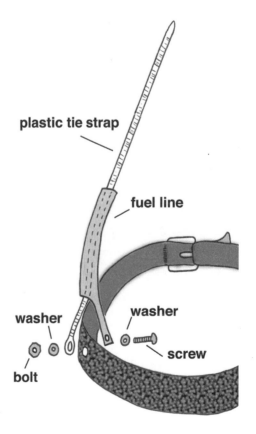

Secure these pieces with the rivet or bolt and washers. If using a screw, place the head of the screw on the inside of the collar and the bolt on the outside. Trim off the excess length of screw and file it smooth. If using rivets, they must fit quite tightly to keep the feelers from drooping. Trim the plastic canes until they extend about 3 inches beyond your dog's nose.

Dogs learn to drag these canes along the wall or floor as a guide. However, dogs can still bump into obstacles thin enough to fit between the canes. For more complete protection, a halo or hoop is needed.

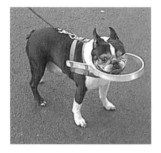

Halos and Hoops

Several dog owners have devised halos or hoops that protrude beyond the dog's chest. These are attached to either a leather harness or fabric vest. The latter is better suited to small dogs. Read the following discussion to help you decide which design may best suit your dog, environment, and your skills as a craftsman.

To Make a Harness

Take the following measurements. (A) Measure the dog's girth. Encircle his body with the measuring tape, just behind his front legs. (B) Measure the distance from the base of his neck to his girth — the spot just behind his front leg. (C) Measure the distance from the base of his neck to his nose. (The other measurements in this diagram will be discussed in following sections.)

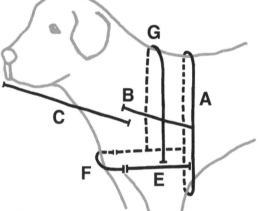

Purchase the following items:

- Some type of flexible material to form
  the hoop or halo: aluminum strips (1 inch wide x 1/16 inch thick) or carpet joining strips (the type *without* gripper teeth) available at a hardware or home improvement store
- Four rivets: 3/16 inch x 1/4 inch or four screws and bolts of similar dimensions; plus eight washers
- A leather harness — leather is preferable but nylon web harnesses may suffice if washers are placed near the drill holes. Use measurement (A) to help you purchase an appropriately sized harness.

The aluminum strip must be of sufficient length to create the circle in front of the dog, as well as the sidepieces that to attach to the vest. One dog owner recommends the following mathematical equation to figure the length needed: Multiply measurement (B) by two. Multiply measurement (C) by four. Add these two sums together. Other dog owners simply "eyeball" the necessary length needed and make some trial cut lengths. Larger dogs require greater lengths. For example, a Labrador Retriever will require an aluminum strip that is approximately 54 inches in length.

Drill or punch a hole at each end of the strip. The holes should be slightly smaller than the screws or rivets and approximately 1/3 inch to 1/2 inch from the ends. (Use larger increment for larger dogs.)

Place the harness on the dog. Measure the distance between the two upright (vertical) strips (D). (See photo at right.) Transfer measurement (D) onto the aluminum strip and drill a second hole at this point. Finish off the ends of the strip by rounding the corners with tin snips or an electric grinder and sandpaper. This will prevent sharp edges from poking the dog.

Photos of blind Boston Terrier, "Axel"
courtesy of Kathy Stefanko

Remove the harness. Drill one hole in *only* the front-most vertical strip of the harness. Place the hole toward the bottom of the strip. (If drilled too high, the hoop will droop excessively.)

Mark measurement (B) at each end of the aluminum. This length will define the section that rests along the dog's side. This is a greater distance than just (D) alone. Gently bend each end of the strip at this point, to a 45-degree angle.

Next, gently round the center section. Finally, place a slight curve in the sidepieces. This will give the dog a more comfortable fit.

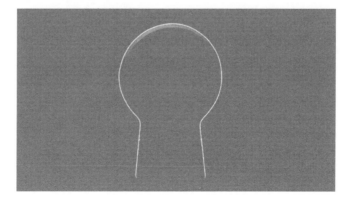

With the rivets (or bolts, washers, and screws) attach the hoop to *only* the front-most vertical bar of the harness. Replace the harness on the dog. Lift the hoop until it is level with the dog's eyes and nose. Mark the spot where the end hole in the hoop hits the back piece of the harness.

Remove the harness. Drill holes at these marks. Only the smooth ends of rivets or bolts should come in contact with the dog. Trim off excessive screw length and file smooth.

Photo courtesy of Shari Burghart

To Make a Fabric Vest

Fabric vests are best suited to small dogs, as fabric cannot support the long length of tubing necessary for large dogs. Fabric vests are available commercially, but since they are handcrafted and custom tailored, there may be a waiting list. (See *Supplier's* section for the "Littlest Angel Vest.") If you are an experienced seamstress/tailor, you may be able to construct one yourself.

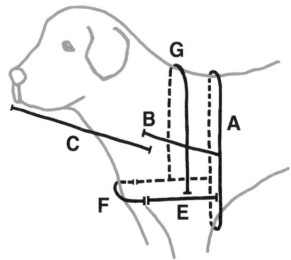

Photo courtesy of Shari Burghart

Purchase the following items:
- Inexpensive fabric from which to experiment and cut a pattern
- Heavy denim fabric for the final product
- Four suspender clips or Velcro strips
- Polyethylene water-line tubing
- Aluminum tubing, small enough to fit inside the polyethylene tubing (usually a length of 2 to 4 feet depending on the size of the dog)
- Medium gauge wire (approximately 2 feet total)

To make a fabric vest, you will need three measurements, in addition to those discussed previously. You will need to measure the distance from the girth to the front of his "arm" (E), the distance across the front of the chest (F), and the distance over the withers, from shoulder joint to shoulder joint (G).

The vest is essentially a wide band of fabric that crosses over the shoulders and is secured by one strap under the chest and another in front of the chest. With the inexpensive fabric, practice and make a pattern using the measurements you have taken. The front strap should equal the following measurements: (E)+(F)+(E). The second strap (under the chest) should equal measurement (A)-(G).

The band over the shoulders is flared at either end and slightly tapered in the middle. This accommodates the dog's shoulders and normal collar. The straps can be secured with Velcro, snaps, or suspender clips (as shown in photo, left). Straps should attach at both ends, making the vest fully adjustable.

Once you have made an appropriate pattern, transfer the pattern onto the denim fabric. Include a hem allowance. Transfer the pattern twice, as the vest requires two layers. *Straps* should be constructed as a tube (turn them inside-out) or folded and hemmed. You may also try the thin webbing designed for making belts.

Hem the edges of both vest pieces.

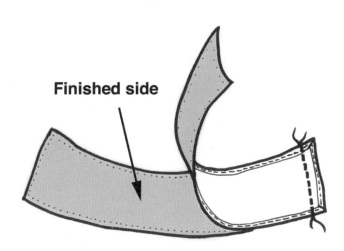

Lay them atop each other, hemmed-side out. Sew together the short ends, only. Turn the vest right side out. Place the vest over the dog's shoulders and using a long straightedge, mark the height at which the halo tubing would protect the dog's nose. Stitch across the vest at the marked spot. This will be the first of four such rows of stitching. Together, they will create channels to keep the halo attached to the vest.

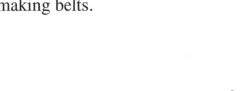

Finished side

Repeat the row of stitching approximately 1/2 inch higher up. This channel must be wide enough to accommodate the poly tubing. Be sure that the tubing will fit inside the channel. Set the tubing near the first row of stitching, lay the fabric over it, and mark the seam accordingly.

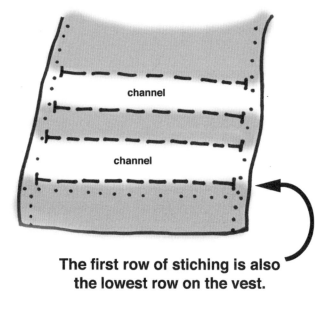

The first row of stiching is also the lowest row on the vest.

Photo courtesy of Shari Burghart

Leave a slight gap between the first channel and the second channel. This is due to the fact that the tubing bends in a U-shape and cannot fold exactly on top of itself. As you stitch rows three and four, creating the second channel, do not stitch to the very edge of the vest. This will give some room to accommodate the curve of the tubing. Finally, stitch up the long sides of the vest, avoiding the channels.

Purchase sufficient polyethylene water-line tubing (at the hardware or home improvement store) to comprise both the halo and the sidepieces that will fold into the channels of the vest. To roughly figure this length, multiply measurement (C) by two. Multiply measurement (F) by four or five. Add these sums together. Experiment. Ultimately, the halo should extend 3 to 4 inches in front of the dog's nose.

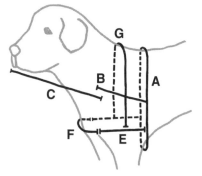

Using the illustration as a guide, cut two pieces of aluminum tubing. These "pegs" will reinforce the poly tubing at the vest and at the beginning of the circle. (The front of the halo is not reinforced with aluminum, permitting flexibility.)

The aluminum pegs should be of sufficient length to fill the lower channel, rest along the dog's side — measurement (E) — and also extend into the halo approximately one-quarter to one-third of the way. Push the aluminum tubing well into the poly tubing, leaving some plain poly tubing at the end. Measure the length of the upper channel on the vest. This is the length of plain poly tubing you will need remaining at the end.

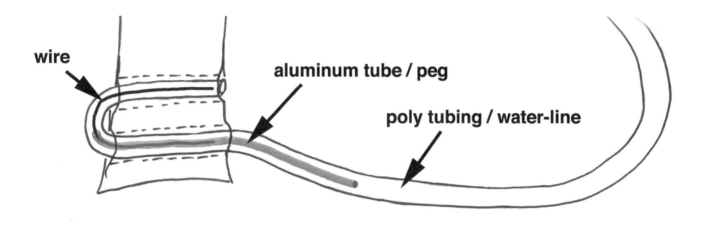

Finally, cut a piece of medium-heavy wire approximately 8 to 12 inches in length. Insert the wire into the end of the poly tubing. The wire will also extend part way into the aluminum peg and prevent it from twisting in the vest. Insert the tubing assembly into the lower channel of the vest until sufficient poly tubing/wire protrudes out the back. Bend this into the upper channel. At the point where the tubing exits the front of the vest, bend the aluminum away from the dog's side in order to create the halo/circle. Attach and adjust suspender clips, Velcro, etc. If you find that you need a firmer design, experiment with a longer aluminum peg, such that it fills both the lower *and upper* channel of the vest.

Photo courtesy of Shari Burghart

Training Dogs to Use Hoops and Halos

Dog owners report that these devices are best used under supervision or when going into unfamiliar territory. Unattended, dogs have been known to get their hoops and halos stuck on furniture or shrubbery. In addition, other pack members may view the apparatus as a toy, engaging the blind dog in an unwanted game of tug-of-war.

Gradually introduce the vest or harness to your dog. Simply put it on and take it off at first. When he is comfortable wearing it, practice the *Go Slowly*. Place your hand against the hoop, apply gentle pressure, and tell him, "E-e-easy." If he slows, reward him. Over several months, the dog should learn to slow when he feels pressure on the sides of the vest or harness.

Monitor him as he moves about. Do not simply "turn him loose" with it. Some dogs may use the hoop to plow down obstacles and other pets. Others may be unsure or even frightened of the device at first.

The owners of large dogs report that the hoop is less helpful indoors (as it is exactly the height, unfortunately, to clear off the coffee table) but extremely helpful outdoors and in new situations, such as hiking in the park.

Other White Canes

Remember that the pipe-leash can also help your dog in unfamiliar territory. Mark the side of the PVC pipe with the words "Blind Dog." Use it to guide your dog at the veterinarian's office, the groomer's, or other public areas.

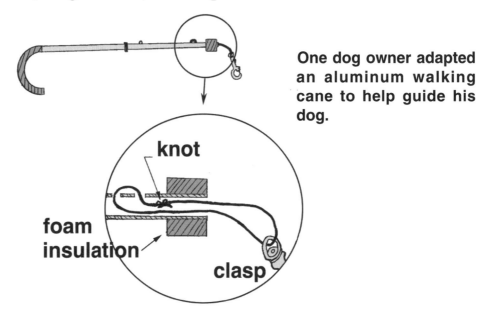

One dog owner adapted an aluminum walking cane to help guide his dog.

knot

foam insulation

clasp

References

Ettelson, R., "White Canes for Blind Dogs," *Off—Lead*, November, 1987.

Higham, D., "Building a Harness and Hoop for a Blind Dog," *http://www.btinternet.com/~dave.higham/ buildaharness.htm*, April 7, 2003.

DOGS BOTH BLIND AND DEAF

Dogs experience hearing loss for a variety of reasons. Some causes include genetic problems, head trauma, chronic infection, and age-related changes. SARD dogs may experience transient hearing loss, along with other symptoms of excess cortisol production.

Some dogs lose all ability to hear, while others may retain limited hearing. These dogs may still respond to sounds such as the oven timer, a train whistle, or another dog's bark. You can experiment at home with different pitches to see if your dog retains any hearing.

You may also have your dog's hearing evaluated by your local veterinarian or tested by a veterinary specialist. In some cases, the hearing loss may be treatable. Eliminating chronic ear infections and minimizing cortisol production can be effective. Hearing aids and some surgical procedures may also improve hearing.

If the onset of deafness is recent, your dog may experience some of the same behavioral changes he did when he lost sight (depression and aggression). Dogs blind and deaf from birth may be more insecure and cry more than other puppies.

You, too, may experience feelings of loss. Remember that dogs take their cues you from you, their pack leader. If your expectations are low, your dog may not have the best chance for a full life.

Dogs that are both blind and deaf do present unique training challenges, however. These dogs cannot rely upon visual cues *or* verbal commands. In these cases, communication will be based on tactile signals, vibration, and scent cues.

As you read this chapter, decide which cues you will use to communicate. Compile a list of the things that you tell your dog on a daily basis. Examples may include: Asking the dog if he needs to go out, or if he wants to go for a walk. You may need to tell him that: Dinner is ready; you are going to pick him up; or that he is a "Good dog!"

Photo of blind Greyhound, "Boomer" courtesy of Lauren Emery

Tactile Cues

There are some basic techniques for dealing with dogs that are both blind and deaf. You must interact more physically with the dog. Many cues and commands can be communicated through touch. Keep training wands in various locations around your home to facilitate communication with small dogs.

Develop a specific cue for each message. A ruffling of fur or hug around the dog's neck can mean, "Good dog!" Slow strokes along the dog's cheek can impart security as in, "It's okay." A hand on his back can mean, "Stop." A couple of gentle taps on his side can mean, "Move aside. I need to walk past you." "Step down" can be communicated by tapping the dog's chest. "Step up" can be communicated by a gentle, upward tug on the dog's collar.

Touch the dog in the same place and in the same manner as you develop each signal. Consistent signals may minimize the dog's tendency to startle. If your dog is especially jumpy, stomp on the floor, blow on his fur, and/or let him smell your hand before touching him. Twitch the edge of his blanket or bedding before waking him.

Vibration Cues

Vibration cues are useful when your dog is too far away for you to reach out and touch him. Vibration can be used to call the dog to you or to have him cease a behavior. Examples of vibration cues include stomping the floor or bouncing a tennis ball. A small radio or metronome turned facedown into the floor boards may also work.

The Vibrating Collar

If you are interested in a high-tech way of communicating with your dog, consider a vibrating collar. These are *not* the electronic shock collars used to train hunting and some obedience dogs. In fact, it's best if there is *no* shock option, as this will eliminate accidental and unintended punishment.

Several models of vibrating collars are available. One is useful to locate a dog that wanders away, but most can be used to communicate with your dog. See *Suppliers* section for listings.

Each collar is basically a radio system — a transmitter and receiver. The collars are fitted with a fabric pouch or small, plastic box that holds a battery-powered vibrator/receiver.

A hand-held transmitter relays the signal to the collar. Introduce your dog to the collar and its vibration as described on page 85.

As with touch commands, various types of vibrations can mean different things. Multiple, short, urgent vibrations can mean, "Wait!" or "Watch out!" A single, medium-length signal can mean, "Sit" or "Stay." One long, continuous vibration may mean, "Search for me until the signal stops" (essentially "Come"). With training, it is possible to communicate with your dog at a distance of a hundred feet or more.

If you are mechanically inclined, construct your own collar. Purchase an inexpensive, remote-controlled (radio) toy car. Search for the type that is normally "off" until the switch is activated. (Some are continually "on" and the switch puts the car in reverse. These are less suitable.) The more basic the car's function, the more cost effective it will be. It may also be possible to purchase the necessary components at a hobby store.

Dismantle the car until you find the electronics assembly. Frequently, this is housed in a plastic casing and includes the battery, electronics, and on/off switch. Remove this assembly from the car.

Next, locate and extract the motor. Glue (epoxy) a small washer or tiny scrap of metal to the shaft of the motor. This will cause it to become unbalanced and vibrate. The larger the metal scrap, the greater the vibration. Evaluate different effects by first taping various sized metal scraps on to the shaft.

Place the motor assembly inside a waterproof nylon pouch or an empty film canister. Pad the empty space with paper or bubble wrap. Secure the electronics assembly to the collar with heavy thread or tape. Secure the antennae onto the collar to prevent it from getting caught in obstacles.

Training Dogs Both Blind and Deaf

While the cues used for blind/deaf dogs may differ, basic training concepts remain the same.

- Show the dog what you want him to do by luring him with food.
- Use a consistent cue to communicate your meaning.
- Heavily reward the dog when he accomplishes the skill.

If you need to gently admonish the dog, use the water squirt bottle.

Teaching the *Recall* might include the following steps: Stomp your foot on the floor three to four times.

Go to the dog and place a food treat under his nose, but do not allow him to eat it. Lure him to the place where you stomped your foot. Reward him with treats.

It might be helpful to routinely call the dog (stomp) from the same spot. If the dog continues to have difficulty finding you, lay down carpet runners and/or scent cues toward this spot.

To teach the *Recall* when the dog is at a distance, use a vibrating collar. Simply substitute the continuous vibration for the continuous sound previously discussed. Once the dog is within close contact, stop the signal and heavily reward him.

Hold down the handpiece button to activate the vibrational cue. Simultaneously, lure the dog toward you with a food treat.

When the dog reaches you, release the button and stop the vibration. Eventually, the dog will search for you until the vibration ends.

The vibrating collar can also be used to teach the dog to stop or wait, thus avoiding injuries. However, unlike the *Recall*, in which one, long signal is used, teach the *Stop* or *Wait* with one to two *short* signals. In addition, it may be necessary to enlist the help of a second person to teach this skill. As one of you gives the physical cue to stop (backward pressure on the chest or collar), the other should give the vibrational cue (one to two short bursts).

Negotiating the House and Yard

In previous chapters we discussed how scent markers (page 100) and tactile pathways (page 102) could be removed once your dog builds a mental map of his environment. In the case of dogs both blind and deaf, it may be best to keep these cues in place for the duration of the dog's life.

Use scent to either help the dog avoid obstacles *or* to find important places such as the back door. Scent the collars of other pack members. Use pots of scented flowers and paths of fresh bark chips to help him navigate the yard.

Use the peanut-butter-on-the-spoon technique if your dog is hesitant to walk on leash or navigate new environments.

A small radio or metronome turned facedown into the floor boards can help the dog locate important places, such as the water bowl, or avoid an obstacle, such as a coffee table.

Games and Activities for Dogs: Both Blind and Deaf

Purchase or scent the dog's balls and other toys. Signal the dog that playtime is about to begin by sliding or rolling the ball along his side or neck. Move to a small, walled area for ball playing. Roll the ball into the walls. Aim so the ball bounces off the wall and gently rolls into your dog. He will find the ball because he can feel it.

Tracking games are excellent activities for dogs that are both blind and deaf. If your dog is elderly, use pungent food treats such as hot dogs or cheese. Tug-of-war games are appropriate for dogs that do not have dominance issues.

Blind and deaf dogs may benefit from being taken on frequent walks. The array of scents will be stimulating. Cue the dog that you are taking him for a walk by letting him smell his leash. If you are able to retrace your steps on the way home, your dog may be able to scent this trail.

Other activities that are good for blind and deaf dogs include chew toys and chew bones. These will provide a safe activity.

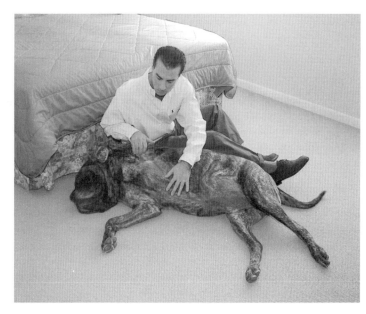

Physical massage may also help the dog remain connected to you and his environment.

If your dog does not clearly indicate that he needs to go out to the yard, hang a string of bells from the doorknob. Using the house training techniques described in Chapter 15. Lead the dog to the door, raise his paw to ring the bell, reward him with a treat, and let him outside. He will not be able to hear the bell, of course, but you will.

DOGS BLIND FROM BIRTH

Puppies that are born blind can elicit a unique reaction from pet lovers — sorrow that the dog will never experience the sense of vision. Interestingly, it is these dogs that usually have the fullest lives. *Not knowing* the sense of vision makes its absence less important. Blind puppies do not realize they are blind. The games and training discussed in previous chapters apply to blind dogs at any stage of life. This chapter will focus on issues specific to puppyhood.

Blind Puppy Behaviors

Blind puppies may exhibit some unique behaviors. One owner describes how her puppy plays by butting into others, as would a goat. Several owners report that their dogs tilt their heads back and sway from side to side when listening for a sound.

Another owner notices an interesting mapping behavior. The puppy moves around the room in widening, concentric circles. He gently bumps into the furniture, mapping the open spaces in between. Once the layout was learned, the behavior stopped.

Photo of blind Border Collie, "Dottie," courtesy of Connie Zamora

Keep training sessions short while dogs are young. A blind puppy should be taught the same manners as the other dogs in your pack. Do not permit him to be obnoxious because you feel sorry for him. Do not allow him to scratch or bite you. Discourage such behavior with the water bottle or a loud "Ouch!" Promptly give the dog an appropriate chew toy and tell him, "Good chew." Keep chew toys located around the house.

House Training Blind Puppies

One of the most successful methods of house training is called "crate training." This method is based on the natural instincts of the dog as a den animal. Dogs tend not to soil the places where they sleep. Since puppies need frequent resting periods, the concept of crate training is valuable on several levels.

To crate train a puppy, purchase or borrow a dog crate. If your dog is a large breed, you may purchase an adult-size crate but place a carton or plastic tub in the rear half. It is important that, initially, the interior be only large enough for the puppy to sleep. If the area is much larger, the puppy will be able to soil one part of the crate, while still sleeping in another part.

Introduce the puppy to the crate by luring him in and out with a treat. Next, toss the treats several inches into the crate and encourage the puppy to get them. Close the door for a few seconds, open it, and reward him. Teach him that the crate is not something to be feared.

Most dogs become very comfortable in their crate, but some puppies cry when first placed inside. Place the puppy in the crate when he is sleepy and ready for a nap. Place a chew toy or a peanut butter stuffed Kong into the crate with him.

Typical Schedule for Crate Training a Puppy

The puppy sleeps overnight in the crate.

7:00 am: Lift the puppy out of the crate and carry him to the yard. (If you try to lead him to the door, odds are good that he will urinate along the way.) While the puppy urinates (outdoors) give a command such as, "Hurry up!" or "Potty." Reward him immediately with a treat. He may or may not have a bowel movement at this time.

7:05 am — 7:15 am: Serve the puppy breakfast. When he is finished, take him back outside to have a bowel movement (BM). Reward him if he does.

7:15 am — 8:00 am: If the puppy relieves himself, he is allowed some free time in a supervised area. This may mean playing in the kitchen as you cook, etc. Cordon off the area so he cannot leave you and mistakenly have an accident elsewhere in the house. At the end of the play period, or if the puppy begins to circle, take the dog outside again. Give the command, reward him if he relieves himself, and place him in the crate for a nap.

8:00 am — 9:00 am: If tired, the puppy will nap. This is an excellent time for you to attend to other things and other dogs.

9:00 am (or when the puppy wakens): Take the puppy outdoors to urinate.

Dogs typically need to eliminate after sleeping, after playing, and after meals. If the puppy does not eliminate when you ask it of him, place him back in the crate.

This cycle will repeat itself over and over during the day. If you work out of the house it would be beneficial for a trusted neighbor or friend to come to the house and let the puppy in and out. Young puppies may only hold their bladder for an hour or less. Puppies that are six months old may be able to hold it for several hours. Having someone let the puppy out during the day increases the chances of successful house training.

To further maximize success, help the dog find his way to the yard. Lay a tactile pathway to the backdoor. Scent the door and the pathway, or place a radio near the door. If you fail to notice when your dog "asks" to go out, install a doggy-door or hang a string of bells by the door. Train the dog to ring the bell when he needs to go out. Raise his paw to ring the bell, reward him with a treat, and let him outside.

Socializing Blind Puppies

With a few exceptions regarding safety (avoiding obstacles), a blind puppy should not be raised differently from other puppies. It is important for the puppy to hear new noises, socialize in new environments, and meet children and other dogs. Take your dog to puppy kindergarten classes to build his confidence.

Photo of blind Poodle puppy, "Snookers," courtesy of John Willmarth

Monitor the puppy's interactions with the older dogs in your pack. If the puppy does not respond to the gentle reprimands of an older dog, the interaction could escalate into one of aggression. This occurs because the puppy cannot read the body language of other dogs. In this case, it may be best to give the older dogs some puppy-free time.

VISION AND THE MODERN-DAY DOG

Medical research continues to uncover numerous connections between lifestyle and health, or more specifically, lifestyle and illness. Several factors contribute to disease, and this includes ophthalmic disease. Contributing factors include stress, genetics, and chemical exposure. And, the simple fact is, the modern-day dog is subjected to more chemicals and physical stress than ever before.

Many people may think of stress as a psychological issue. There are other types of stress, however. Chronic irritation is a very destructive form of stress. When we examine the anatomy and physiology of the canine body, it becomes increasingly clear that the modern-day lifestyle may cause our pets chronic irritation. Diet is a leading offender.

Diet

Most commercial pet foods consist mainly of grain products. These are not biologically appropriate for the dog. Canine nutritionists explain that dogs are poorly designed to digest grain and that diets high in grain irritate the gastrointestinal (GI) tract. Chronic, low-grade irritation can cause difficulty in absorbing fat-soluble vitamins and fatty acids. These nutrients are necessary for proper retinal function. In addition, studies on humans link grain protein to autoimmune and endocrine (hormone) diseases.

Highly processed diets are laden with chemical additives. Examples include dyes, preservatives, texturizers, stabilizers, thickeners, clay products, flavorings, as well as binding, drying, and anti-caking agents. Highly processed diets do not contain any fresh foods. They place a heavy workload on the pancreas, the organ that produces digestive enzymes. This can lead to pancreatic inflammation and slowed digestion, allowing substantial time for chemicals to further irritate the GI tract. These various sources of irritation contribute to increased production of cortisol, the stress hormone.

Excess cortisol is damaging in myriad ways. It damages retinal and brain cell membranes, including those in the hypothalamus. This area of the brain controls appetite, temperature control, and mood. Consequently, dogs producing excess cortisol are often hungry, thirsty, depressed, or heat intolerant (pant). Excess cortisol contributes to insomnia, incontinence, and seizures. It breaks down body fat resulting in high levels of triglycerides and cholesterol. It pulls calcium from bones and cartilage and deposits it into soft tissue such as the skin, lungs, bladder, and cornea. Cortisol depresses the immune system, resulting in more frequent infections.

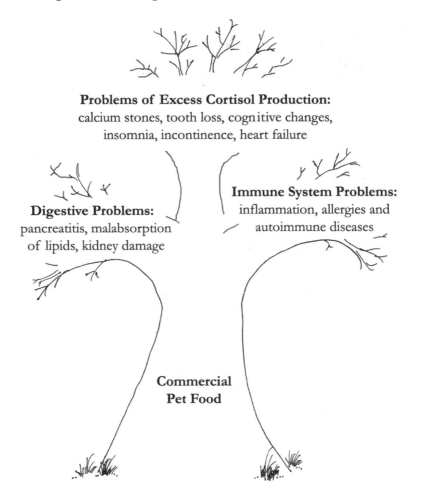

Problems of Excess Cortisol Production:
calcium stones, tooth loss, cognitive changes,
insomnia, incontinence, heart failure

Digestive Problems:
pancreatitis, malabsorption
of lipids, kidney damage

Immune System Problems:
inflammation, allergies and
autoimmune diseases

**Commercial
Pet Food**

Recently, researchers have realized the connection between excess cortisol and **genetic diseases**. Excess cortisol crosses cell membranes and affects the DNA material found there. It "turns on" or activates portions of the DNA strand that have previously been kept dormant. In this way, genetic predispositions begin to express themselves.

A wide variety of ophthalmic, autoimmune, and endocrine diseases are considered to have a genetic basis. The list is long and includes progressive retinal atrophy, primary glaucoma, uveodermatologic or Vogt-Koyanagi-Harada syndrome, type I diabetes mellitus, keratoconjunctivitis sicca, primary epilepsy, hereditary cataracts, and retinal dysplasia, to name a few.

Vaccines and Chemicals

In addition to an irritating diet and genetic predispositions, several other factors are believed to contribute to immune system failure. Over-vaccination is one of these. For years, the practice has been to inoculate pets on an annual basis. This repeatedly and unnecessarily provokes the immune response, which includes the release of cortisol. Presently, veterinarians are departing from the practice of annual vaccines. If you have an adult pet (older than three or four years of age), it is likely that he has developed lifelong immunity to the diseases for which he's been inoculated.

Chemicals and pesticides are also elements of modern-day life. Many of the pesticides we use on our pets are neurotoxins. They damage nerve cell function in order to kill the insect. Many of these pesticides are also lipophilic. They are attracted to tissues high in lipid (fat) content, such as retinal cell membranes. In fact, the retina is a common site of chemical accumulation.

Another Approach

While you may pursue traditional treatments for your dog's vision loss (such as medication, surgery, and training), there may also be value in providing your dog with a more natural lifestyle. This includes three main issues: Feeding a more wholesome diet; avoiding over-vaccination: and reducing the chemical load faced by the dog. These are sound concepts to reduce inflammation, reduce cortisol production, and improve general health and longevity.

Since a detailed discussion of these topics is beyond the scope of this book, please see page 184 for details on *Dogs, Diet, and Disease*, another resource book by the author.

References

Blaylock, R.L., *Excitotoxins: The Taste That Kills*. Santa Fe: Health Press, 1994.

Carmody, R.J., and Cotter, T.G., "Oxidative Stress Induces Caspase-independent Retinal Apoptosis in Vitro," *Cell Death Differentiation,* 7(3): March, 2000.

Claudio, L., et al, "Testing Methods for Developmental Neurotoxicity of Environmental Chemicals," *Toxicology and Applied Pharmacology*, 164(1): April, 2000.

Collin, P., Kaukinen, K., Valimaki, M., and Salmi, J., "Endocrinological Disorders and Celiac Disease," *Endocrine Review,* 23(4): August, 2002.

Councell, C., et al, "Coexistence of Celiac and Thyroid Disease," *Gut,* 35(6): June, 1994.

Grabenstein, J.D., *Immuno Facts: Vaccines & Immunologic Drugs.* St. Louis: Facts & Comparisons, 1999.

Gulcan, H.G., Alvarez, R.A., Maude, M.B., Anderson, R.E., "Lipids of Human Retina, Retinal Pigment Epithelium, and Bruch's Membrane/Choroid: Comparison of Macular and Peripheral Regions," *Investigative Ophthalmology and Visual Science*, 34(11): October, 1993.

Hughes, G.R.V., "The Antiphospholipid Syndrome: Ten Years On," *Lancet*, 342: August, 1993.

Levin, C.D., *Dogs, Diet, and Disease: An Owner's Guide to Diabetes Mellitus, Pancreatitis, Cushing's Disease, and More.* Oregon City: Lantern Publications, 2001.

Olson, L., "Anatomy of a Carnivore and Dietary Needs," *B-Natural's Newsletter,* Spring, 1999.

Raber, J., "Detrimental Effects of Chronic Hypothalamic-Pituitary-Adrenal Axis Activation," *Molecular Neurobiology*, August, 1998.

Rosenberger, B., *Life Itself: Exploring the Realm of the Living Cell.* Oxford: Oxford Press, 1998.

Sapolsky, R.M., *Why Zebras Don't Get Ulcers: An Updated Guide to Stress, Stress Related Disease, and Coping.* New York: W.H. Freeman & Co., 1998.

Sarjeant, D., and Evans, K., *Hard to Swallow: The Truth About Food Additives.* Burnaby, BC: Alive Books, 1999.

Scott, D.W., Miller, W.H., and Griffin, C.E., *Muller & Kirk's Small Animal Dermatology.* Philadelphia: W.B. Saunders Co., 2000.

Strombeck, D.R., *Home Prepared Dog & Cat Diets: The Healthful Alternative.* Ames: Iowa State University Press, 1999.

United States Congress Office of Technology Assessment, *Fundamentals of Neurotoxicology*, 1990.

Closing Thoughts

Even with all the information in this book, you may have experiences that frustrate you. This is entirely normal. So, in these final comments, I would like to offer you encouragement.

Experienced dog trainers have made the following observations:

- You will have some good training sessions in which your dog will make progress and you will feel happy.
- You will have some bad training sessions in which your dog will not make progress and you may feel frustrated. (Don't let the dog know, though.)
- You will make some mistakes in your training.
- There may be days that you feel like giving up.
- There may be exercises that you don't practice because they are difficult or because you don't like them.

To these I would add:

- Be patient and keep trying. Your dog needs you. Owners repeatedly explain that it takes time for dogs to learn these new skills.

With the broad background provided to you in this book, you'll have a good understanding of canine behavior and dog-training theory. Use this knowledge to modify the exercises explained herein or to develop new skills particular to your environment. This book provides a solid foundation.

Norman, the Hero Dog

Finally, I'd like to tell you a story.

The summer of 1996 was an unusually warm one in the Pacific Northwest. Sightseers and residents alike flocked to the rugged and usually bleak Oregon coastline. It was so warm that year, children even ventured into the cool ocean waters.

One popular swimming spot was at the mouth of the Necanicum River, where it enters the Pacific. This broad expanse of river made for an inviting playground. Here, the water was smooth in comparison to the crashing surf beyond it, but it belied a deadly secret: As water flowed from the Necanicum into the Pacific, strong and unexpected currents were created.

Norman, a yellow Labrador Retriever, and his owner, Annette, frequently took trips to the beach. Like many other days, Annette was tending to her young son and Norman was gleefully running along the shoreline carrying a stick in his mouth. He loved the wide-open expanse of the beach.

Unexpectedly, Norman dropped his stick, ran into the water, and started swimming straight out to deep sea. Annette, initially confused by this, quickly became frantic. She didn't know what Norman was doing, where he was going, or even, if he could swim! She called and called his name but he continued swimming away from her.

Then Annette became aware of something else. What she had thought were the joyful noises of children at play were really cries for help. A teenage girl and her younger brother had been playing in the water. Both of the children were actually very capable swimmers, but the Necanicum had become too much for them. The boy was able to make it to shore, but his sister needed help.

Annette realized what was happening. Norman must have recognized the urgent pitch in the girl's voice and was swimming to help her. Annette shouted to the girl, "His name is Norman! Call his name!" The swimmer caught a glimpse of the dog coming toward her, and called out to him.

Norman followed the sound of the girl's voice and swam to her. She grabbed the thick fur of his ruff and together they headed toward shore. Annette let out a sigh of relief. Everything seemed fine until the girl lost her grip and quickly became separated from Norman.

Annette hollered again, "Call his name! His name is Norman!" Again, the girl did as she was told, and she and dog caught up with each other. Finally, after what had seemed like hours, they made it to the beach.

This is a wonderful and touching story, but there's more to it. What makes it truly amazing is that Annette and her husband, Steve, had adopted Norman from the local animal shelter the day before he was scheduled for euthanasia. Even more extraordinary than that, though, was the fact that Norman had been suffering from progressive retinal atrophy for the past two years. He was completely blind when he saved this girl from certain drowning.

When Norman started losing his vision, friends told Annette and Steve to have the dog euthanized. They were so glad they didn't listen. The same was obviously true for the children swimming in the ocean that day.

Blind dogs can live happy and useful lives.

Photo of blind Labrador Retriever, "Norman," courtesy of Annette McDonald

Suppliers and Resources

If you are having difficulty locating toys and training aids at your local pet supply store, you may be able to order them from catalogues. The following list includes suppliers located in the United States of America, the United Kingdom, Canada, and Australia.

To order:

Metronomes for placing inside toys, on furniture, or near doors (the smallest model is the Seiko DM33 clip-on metronome at 1.5" x 2")

Contact:
Teachers Discount Music
PO Box 390
New Market, VA 22844
Telephone: 800-586-3876
Fax: 540-740-3741
Web site: www.metronomes.net

To order:

waterproof, plastic cell-phone cases that protect metronomes during water play

Contact:
Waterproof Cases.net
7900-20 103rd Street, Suite 47
Jacksonville, FL 32210
Telephone: 877-789-5255
Web site: www.waterproofcases.net

To order:

Doggles, UV **protected eyewear (goggles)** for dogs; leashes and collars

Contact:
Doggles
Midknight Creations
107 South Mary Avenue #61
Sunnyvale, CA 94086
Telephone: 408-735-1220
Web site: www.doggles.com

To order:

The Littlest Angel **Blind Dog Vest**, a fabric vest and plastic halo to help small dogs avoid obstacles (The vest was first designed and produced in July of 1999 by Sharilyn H. Burghart. It is dedicated to the memory of her dog, "Scooter", a Miniature Schnauzer, blind from cataracts.) Also available: visors and protective eye masks

Contact:
Shari Burghart
9137 Rockefeller Lane
Springfield, VA 22153
Web site: www.angelvest.homestead.com/

To order:

carting harnesses with D-rings on each side, suitable for you to attach a double-ended leash or U-shaped handle with which to guide a large or medium-sized dog

Contact:
Fidogear
1293 NW Wall #1485
Bend, OR 97701
Telephone: 541-382-2636
Fax 541-617-1207
Web site: www.fidogear.com

To order::

the **PitBall**, a self-contained ball game

Photo courtesy of Gary Bessette

Contact:
Puppy Play Ground
1211 Golf Avenue
Ormond Beach, FL 32174
Telephone: 1-888-828-3416
Web site: www.puppyplayground.com/pitball/index.html

To order::

books and **videos** on highly motivational, competitive **dog training theory** and day-to-day **pack leadership issues** (*Simply Living*). Classes, seminars, and theory developed and presented by Dawn Jecs, nationally recognized obedience/agility instructor, competitor, and lecturer.

Contact:
Choose to Heel
10409 Canyon Road E.
Suite 263
Puyallup, WA 98373
Web site: http://www.choosetoheel.com

To order:

life jackets (personal floatation devices or PFD's) designed specifically for dogs

Contact:
Teeft K-9 Equipment
10 Ilsley Avenue (Unit# 9)
Dartmouth, Nova Scotia, **Canada** B3B-1L3
Telephone: 1-877-286-7141
Fax: 902-446-4067
Web site: www.Teeft.com

To order:

the Soft Quick Lift, a fleece-lined **body sling to carry animals**

Contact:
Four Flags Over Aspen, Inc.
P.O. Box 190
St. Clair, MN 56080
Telephone: 1-800-222-9263
Website: http//www.fourflags.com/FFOA-3html#fleece

To order::
a wide variety of **mats, plastic and fabric runners** for the floor

Contact:

>Commercial Matting
>Consolidated Plastics Company, Inc.
>8181 Darrow Road
>Twinsburg, OH 44087
>Telephone: 1-800-362-1000
>Fax: 216-425-3333
>Web site: www.consolidatedplastics.com

To order:
Ramps and **steps** (for getting on and off of furniture and in and out of cars)

Contact:

I.Q. Industries, Inc.
737 Park Avenue
New York, NY 10021
Telephone: 1-877-364-5438
Web site: www.dogramp.com/index2.html

Or: BedderBacks by Smith-Kruger Inc.
Seal Beach, CA
Telephone: 877-327-5438
Web site: www.bedderbacks.com

Or: Dogbedworks
8 Omaha Avenue
Northboro, MA 01532
Telephone: 1-877-393-3677
Web site: www.dogbedworks.com

Or: C&D Pet Products
405 East D Street
Petaluma, CA 94952
Telephone: 1-888-554-7387
Web site: www.cdpets.com

To order::
beeping balls, toys and other **beeping tools** originally designed for blind humans: *Hide and Seek Talking Cat* plush toy, *EverBounce™ Ball* with internal bell, *Sportime Volley DuraBeep Ball* that beeps, *Key Locator* and *Now You Can Find It (Locator)* to locate a lost dog, *MotionPad* and *Forget-Me Not Motion Activated Message Announcer,* which play a recorded message when the dog approaches

Contact:

>Independent Living Aids
>200 Robbins Lane
>Jericho, NY 11753
>Telephone: 1-800-537-2118
>Fax: 516-937-3906
>Web site: www.independentliving.com/frame_cando.htm

To order:

tab leashes and **retractable leashes,** leather **buckle collars, prong** collars, **head halters,** tracking **harnesses** and **long lines, chew toys,** the **Buster Cube, "Kong"** toys, **scented tennis balls,** toys with **bells, "Yapples"** (rubber balls with holes for peanut butter), and **"Look Who's Talking"** (or **"Chatterbox" toys** in the U.K.), **Hol-ee Roler/Floater** balls, **treat pouches,** training **wands, clickers,** hunting-dog **bells, retrieving dummies, musk oil** scents, **pet beds** (safe spots), **ex-pens,** safety baby **gates, crates, doggy-doors** and black rubber non-skid **mats** to place in front of them, **sun-visors, life preservers,** and **housebreaking pads.**

Contact:

J and J Dog Supplies
P.O. Box 1517
Galesburg, IL 61402
Telephone: 1-800-642-2050
Fax: 309-344-3522
Web site: www.jandjdog.com

Or:

J-B Wholesale Pet Supplies Inc.
5 Raritan Road
Oakland, NJ 07436
Telephone: 1-800-526-0388
Fax: 1-800-788-5005
Web site: www.jbpet.com/

Or:

New England Serum Company
Groomer/Kennel Products Division
P.O. Box 128
Topsfield, MA 01983
Telephone: 1-800-637-3786
Fax: 1-800-329-6372
Web site: www.neserum.com

Or:

Doctors Foster & Smith, Inc.
2253 Air Park Road
Rhinelander, WI 54501-0100
Telephone: 1-800-826-7206
Fax: 1-800-776-8872
Web site: www.drsfostersmith.com

In **Canada**:

Canine Cravings Emporium
999 York Road
Guelph, Ontario, Canada N1E 6Y9
Telephone: 1-800-268-3716
Fax: 519-767-9991
Web site: www.petsupplyhouse.com

In **Australia**:

Perfect Paws Pty. Ltd.
P.O. Box 533
Hillarys, Western Australia 6923
Telephone: 1300 302 779
Fax: 1300 302 778
Web site: www.perfectpaws.com.au/

In the **United Kingdom**:

Champion Pet Supplies
8 Horeston Grange Shopping Centre
Camborne Drive, Nuncaton Warks
United Kingdom CV11 6GU
Telephone: 024 7635 4304
Web site: www.championpetsonline.co.uk

To order:

vibrating collars: some for *training*, others for *locating* a deaf dog

Contact:

Unique Distributors for *Innotek's LCC-100 Cat Locator*
5401 South Siesta Lane
Tempe, AZ 85283
Telephone: 1-800-333-4793
Web site: www.uniquedistributors.com (search site for "*locator*")

Or: ProperPet for *Innotek's VC-100A Pet Call Vibrating Training Collar*
13414 A Street
Omaha, NE 68144
Telephone: 1-877-673-7738
Web site: www.properpet.com

Or: Radio Fence Distributors, Inc. for *Pet Pager Remote Trainer PVPP-300*
1133 Bal Harbor Blvd, Suite 1151
Punta Gorda FL 33950
Telephone: 1-800-941-4200
Web site: http://radiofence.com

In the **United Kingdom**:

Ultimate Animals for *Pet Pager - Vibrating Collar*
Beech View Parade
Walshes Road
Crowborough, East Sussex
United Kingdom TN6 3RA
Telephone: 01892 667733
Web site: www.thingsfor-pets.co.uk

To order:

The **Handler Collar**, which has a leather **handle built onto it**

Contact:

Locke Pet Supply
P.O. Box 303
Alhambra, CA 91802
Telephone: 323-779-6518
Fax: 323-757-9178
Web site: www.lockepet.net

To order:

dog books on puppy training, behavioral problems, tracking, and scent games; and via their affiliation with a company called 3C's: **clickers, training wands** (also called target sticks) and **treat pouches**

Contact:

Dogwise.
701-B Poplar
P.O. Box 2778
Wenatchee, WA 98807-2778
Telephone: 1-800-776-2665
Web site: www.dogwise.com

Additional Resources

To order::

The book *Ocular Disorders Presumed to be Inherited in Dogs* by the Genetics Committee of the American College of Veterinary Ophthalmologists

Contact:

Canine Eye Registration Foundation (CERF)
Purdue University — Lynn Hall
625 Harrison Street
West Lafayette, IN 47907-2026
Telephone: 765-494-8179
Fax: 765-494-9981
Web site: www.vmdb.org/order_j98.html

For information on:
genetic testing

Contact:

OptiGen®, LLC
Cornell Business & Technology Park
767 Warren Road, Suite 300
Ithaca, NY 14850
Telephone: 607-257-0301
Web site: www.optigen.com

Glossary

aa – notation used to denote a gene pair made up of two recessive genes

Aa – notation used to denote a gene pair made up of one recessive gene and one dominant gene

AA – notation used to denote a gene pair comprised of two dominant genes

adrenal glands – endocrine glands that secret cortisol and other hormones

alpha – in this case, the primary or dominant member of a group of animals

anophthalmia – a congenital condition in which the eyes are not present

anterior chamber – the portion of the eye between the cornea and the posterior lens capsule

aqueous humor – fluid produced in the anterior chamber that maintains shape and nourishes the cornea

atrophy – shrinking or withering

auditory markers – sounds that identify the location of various items

beta – in this case, the second most dominant member of a group of animals

bilateral – on both sides

carrier – an individual who does not exhibit signs of a genetic defect but could contribute to producing the defect in any offspring

cataracts – a condition caused by opacity in the lens

choroid – one of the structures lining the back of the eye, comprised of blood vessels

ciliary body – the structure located behind the iris that produces aqueous humor

cognitive mapping – the ability to produce and retain a mental image of a physical area

collie eye anomaly – a hereditary condition causing various congenital malformations of the eye

cones – nerve cells located on the retina that are responsible for color and fine discrimination vision

cornea – the clear structure at the front of the eye which allows light to pass farther into the eye

correction – applying punitive measures (punishment) in an attempt to diminish undesirable behaviors

cortisol – the hormone secreted during mental stress, pain, and physical irritation

cryotherapy – a surgical procedure that uses liquid nitrogen to freeze tissue

cues – signs and signals given to the dog that assist him in performing a desired behavior

Diabetes mellitus – a metabolic disorder in which the body does not produce adequate insulin, a substance necessary to process sugar

electroretinogram (ERG) – a medical test that measures the electrical function of the retina

enucleation – complete surgical removal of the eyeball with the eyelids sutured together

evisceration – surgical removal of the internal contents of the eye, leaving the external eyebal intact

filtration angle – the structure that acts as the "drainage field" through which aqueous humor escapes, located just anteriorly to the iris, along the wall of the eye

glaucoma – a condition of fluid accumulation and excess pressure in the eye; left untreated, it can result in pain and irreversible blindness

hemorrhage – massive or uncontrolled bleeding

hypoxia – insufficient oxygenation

incomplete dominance – a pattern in which two faulty genes cause a disease in its fullest form; and one faulty gene causes the disease to a slighter degree

intraocular – that which is *inside* the eye

iris – the structure in the eye that acts as a diaphragm, constricting and dilating in response to light

ischemia – insufficient blood supply

keratoconjunctivitis sicca (KCS) – dry eye syndrome

lens – the structure that helps to focus light upon the retina

merle ocular dysgenesis – congenital malformations of the eye associated with the merle coat trait

micro-ophthalmia – a congenital condition in which the eyes are small or incompletely developed

ophthalmology – the study of the anatomy and physiology of the eye

pituitary gland – the master endocrine gland

posterior chamber – the portion of the eye from the back of the lens to the retina

progressive retinal atrophy (PRA) or degeneration (PRD) – the common terms used to describe diseases that result in thinning retinal cells

pupil – the opening in the center of the iris

PVC / polyvinyl chloride – white, rigid plastic used for plumbing pipes

recall – training the dog to come when called

release – a term used signify to the dog that he completed his job

retina – the structure comprised of rod and cone cells that sends visual information to the brain

retinal detachment – the separation of the retina from the back wall of the eye

retinal dysplasia – a disease in which the retina is congenitally malformed into folds and puckers, which can result in retinal detachment and blindness

retinal pigment epithelial degeneration – central deterioration of the rods and cones, recently linked to difficulty metabolizing vitamin E

rods – nerve cells of the retina that are responsible for low-light vision and detection of movement

scent marking – using fragrance to identify the location of various items

sclera – the white, fibrous structure that comprises the wall of the eye

simple dominance – a pattern in which two faulty genes must be present for the disease to be present

socialize – the healthy and beneficial act of exposing a dog to multiple stimuli and experiences; most effective if done at an early age (puppyhood)

sub-alpha – a position in the pack order below the alpha position

sudden aquired retinal deterioration (SARD) – a condition in which the retinal cells suddenly atrophy

tactile markers – textures that identify the location of various items

tapetum – one of the structures lining the back of the canine eye that acts to reflect and amplify light

uveitis – inflammation of the uvea, which is comprised of the iris, ciliary body, and choroid together

uveodermatologic syndrome – an autoimmune attack on pigmented tissue

Vogt-Koyanagi-Harada (VKH) syndrome – renamed uveodermatologic syndrome

vitreous humor – gelatinous material filling the posterior chamber of the eye

Bibliography

American College of Veterinary Ophthalmologists, *Ocular Disorders Presumed to be Inherited in Dogs.* West Lafayette: Canine Eye Registration Foundation, 1996.

Anderson, R., and Wrede, B., *Caring for Older Cats & Dogs.* Charlotte: Williamson Publishing, 1990.

Bauman, D.L., *Beyond Basic Dog Training.* New York: Howell Books, 1991.

Blaylock, R.L., *Excitotoxins: The Taste That Kills.* Santa Fe: Health Press, 1994.

Brooks, D.E., Garcia, G.A., Dreyer, E.B., et al, "Vitreous Body Glutamate Concentrations in Dogs with Glaucoma," *American Journal of Veterinary Research*, 58: 1997.

Carmody, R.J., and Cotter, T.G., "Oxidative Stress Induces Caspase-independent Retinal Apoptosis in Vitro," *Cell Death Differentiation,* 7(3): March, 2000.

Claudio, L., et al, "Testing Methods for Developmental Neurotoxicity of Environmental Chemicals," *Toxicology and Applied Pharmacology*, 164(1): April, 2000.

Collin, P., Kaukinen, K., Valimaki, M., and Salmi, J., "Endocrinological Disorders and Celiac Disease," *Endocrine Review,* 23(4): August, 2002.

Councell, C., et al, "Coexistence of Celiac and Thyroid Disease," *Gut,* 35(6): June, 1994.

Cutolo, M., and Wilder, R., "Different Roles for Androgens and Estrogens in the Susceptibility to Autoimmune Rheumatic Diseases," *Rheumatic Diseases Clinics of North America*, 26: 2000.

Donahue, D.J., "The Sightless Dog," *Dog Fancy Magazine*, February, 1996.

Ettelson, R., "White Canes for Blind Dogs," *Off—Lead*, November, 1987.

Field, T., "Massage Therapy," *Medical Clinics of North America*, 86(1): January, 2002.

Grabenstein, J.D., *Immuno Facts: Vaccines & Immunologic Drugs.* St. Louis: Facts & Comparisons, 1999.

Gulcan, H.G., Alvarez, R.A., Maude, M.B., Anderson, R.E., "Lipids of Human Retina, Retinal Pigment Epithelium, and Bruch's Membrane/Choroid: Comparison of Macular and Peripheral Regions,"*Investigative Ophthalmology and Visual Science*, 34(11): October, 1993.

Higham, D., "Building a Harness and Hoop for a Blind Dog," *http://www.btinternet.com/~dave.higham/ buildaharness.htm*, April 7, 2003.

Horger, B.A., and Roth, R.H., "Stress and Central Amino Acid System," *Neurobiological and Clinical Consequences of Stress: From Adaptation to PTSD.* Lippincott-Raven: Philadelphia, 1995.

Hughes, G.R.V., "The Antiphospholipid Syndrome: Ten Years On," *Lancet,* 342: August, 1993.

Jecs, D., *Choose to Heel, the First Steps*: An Innovative Dog Training Manual. Puyallup, Washington: Self-published, 1995.

Jerison, H., *The Evolution of the Brain and Intelligence.* Academic Press, 1973.

Kidd, Parris M., *Phosphatidylserine: The Nutrient Building Block That Accelerates All Brain Functions and Counters Alzheimer's.* New Cannan, Connecticut: Keats Publishing, Inc., 1998.

Kübler-Ross, E., *On Death and Dying.* London: The Macmillan Company, 1969.

Kumar, R., Lumsden, A. J., Ciclitira, P. J., Ellis, H. J., Laurie, G. W., "Human genome search in Celiac disease using gliadin c-DNA as probe," *Journal of Molecular Biology*, 300(5): 2000.

Lechin, F., van der Dijs, B., Lechin, A.E., Orozco, B., Lechin, M.E., Baez, S., et al, "Plasma Neurotransmitters and Cortisol in Chronic Illness: Role of Stress." *Journal of Medicine*, 25: 1994.

Levin, C.D., *Dogs, Diet, and Disease: An Owner's Guide to Diabetes Mellitus, Pancreatitis, Cushing's Disease, and More.* Oregon City: Lantern Publications, 2001.

McLellan, G.J., Elks, R., Lybaert, P., Watté, C., Moore, D., and Bedford, P. G.C., "Vitamin E Deficiency in Canine Retinal Pigment Epithelial Dystrophy," *Veterinary Record*, 151: 2002.

Nickells, R.W., "Retinal Ganglion Cell Death in Glaucoma: The How, the Why and the Maybe," *Journal of Glaucoma*, 123(6): 1996.

Nieman, L.K., "Diagnostic Tests for Cushing's Syndrome," *Annals of the New York Academy of Sciences*, 970: September, 2002.

Nockels, C.F., Odde, K.G., and Craig, A.M., "Vitamin E. Supplementation and Stress Affect Tissue Alpha-tocopherol Content of Beef Heifers," *Journal of Animal Science*, 74(3): 1996.

Olson, L., "Anatomy of a Carnivore and Dietary Needs," *B-Natural's Newsletter,* Spring, 1999.

Optigen staff, "Testing for (Old English) Mastiff and Bullmastiff Dominant PRA," *http://www.optigen.com*, April 28, 2003.

Plechner, A., Zucker, M., Pets at Risk: From *Allergies to Cancer, Remedies for an Unsuspected Epidemic*, Troutdale, Oregon: New Sage Press, 2003.

Raber, J., "Detrimental Effects of Chronic Hypothalamic-Pituitary-Adrenal Axis Activation," *Molecular Neurobiology*, August, 1998.

Rosenberger, B., *Life Itself: Exploring the Realm of the Living Cell*. Oxford: Oxford Press, 1998.

Ross, C.B., and Baron-Sorensen, J., *Veterinarian's Guide to Counseling Grieving Clients*. Lenexa: Veterinary Medicine Publishing Company, 1994.

Sapolsky, R.M., *Why Zebras Don't Get Ulcers: An Updated Guide to Stress, Stress Related Disease, and Coping*. New York: W.H. Freeman & Co., 1998.

Sarjeant, D., and Evans, K., *Hard to Swallow: The Truth About Food Additives*. Burnaby, British Columbia: Alive Books, 1999.

Scott, D.W., Miller, W.H., and Griffin, C.E., *Muller & Kirk's Small Animal Dermatology*. Philadelphia: W.B. Saunders Co., 2000.

Slatter, D., *Fundamentals of Veterinary Ophthalmology*. Philadelphia: W. B. Saunders Company, 2001.

Strombeck, D.R., *Home Prepared Dog & Cat Diets: The Healthful Alternative*. Ames: Iowa State University Press, 1999.

Zigler, M., "Sudden Acquired Retinal Degeneration," *http://www.eyevet.info/sards.html*, April 22, 2003.

Index

H

Halos 140
Hand cues 91
Harnesses 64, 140
Head protection 137
Hearing loss 23, 74, 147
Hoops 140
Hot tubs 110
House training 154, **156**
Humor 118
Hungarian Puli 18

I

IgA. *See* Immunoglobulins
Immunoglobulins 24
Immunology and Endocrinology panel 24
Incontinence 23, 34, **112**
Infections 160
    Bacterial, Viral 34
Insomnia 23
Intraocular pressure (IOP) 9, 28
    Spikes in 9
Introducing
    Dogs 53, 119
    New people 117
    Training equipment 68, **85**
Iris 8, *27*
    dilated 16, 32
Irish Setter 16

J

Jecs, Dawn 53

K

Kennel 54, 108
Keratoconjunctivitis Sicca (KCS) 14
Kübler-Ross, Elisabeth 1

L

Labrador Retriever 16, 18, 26, 31
Laser surgery 26, 29
Leashes 66, 72
    Pipe-leash 87
    Walking a blind dog 85
Lens 8, 31
Lens luxation 27, 41
Leptospirosis 34
Lighting 99, 115
Liver dysfunction 18
Loss 1
    Acceptance 4
    Anger 2
    Bargaining 3

Children, and 5
Denial 2
Depression 3, 45

M

Massage 45, 153
Mats 104
Menace response 13
Mental mapping 76, 105, 116
Methazolamide 29
Metronomes 104
Micro-ophthalmia 34
Miniature Poodle 16, 27, 31
Miniature Schnauzer 16, 31
Moving / New Homes 107
MSG 21. *See* Diet: Commercial pet food: Additives
Mucous discharge 14
Muscle weakness 23, 103

N

Neurotoxins 161
Neurotransmitters 10
New home 107
Newspaper 81
Nitric oxide 28
Norwegian Elkhound 16, 27
Nutrition 21

O

Ocular Disorders Presumed to be Inherited in Dogs 37
Old English Sheepdog 31
"Only" dog 124, 136
Oppositional reflex 89
Optic nerve 10
optic nerve 24
Optimmune 14
Oxidative stress 20, 28

P

Pacing 23, 28
Pack Issues **47**
    Body language 49
    Dominance / submission 48, 51, 119
    Leadership 49, 147
Padding 107
Pain 28, 30
Pancreas 21
Panting 23, 28
Papillion 16
Parasites 34
Pathways 102, 110
Persistent hyperplastic primary vitreous 42
Pesticides 22, 24, 161

Notes

Books by the Author

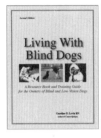

Living With Blind Dogs: A Resource Book and Training Guide for the Owners of Blind and Low-Vision Dogs*,* second edition

8.5" x 11" paperback, 188 pp., illustrated, ISBN 0-9672253-4-5

Helpful hints from hundreds of blind-dog owners. Topics include: Dealing with loss, causes of blindness, how dogs react to blindness, pack interactions, helping dogs negotiate the house, yard, and community; training new skills, toys, games, and more.

Price: $29.95 plus shipping & handling $5.95 (U.S. & Canada)

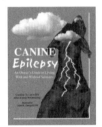

Blind Dogs Stories: Tales of Triumph Humor and Heroism

5.5" x 8.5" paperback, 100 pp., illustrated, ISBN 0-9672253-1-0

Two-dozen heartwarming, short stories from around the world illustrating that blind dogs can live useful, happy lives, offering encouragement to owners, and celebrating the beauty of the human-canine bond.

Price: $12.95 plus shipping & handling $5.95 (U.S. & Canada)

Dogs, Diet, and Disease: An Owner's Guide to Diabetes Mellitus, Pancreatitis, Cushing's Disease, and More

8.5" x 11" paperback, 181 pp., illustrated, ISBN 0-9672253-2-9

Maxwell Award winner: **Best Healthcare Book***!* In-depth instructions to help owners care for chronically ill dogs. Discusses numerous metabolic, digestive, endocrine, and immune system processes. Details insulin injections, treatments for Cushing's and SARD dogs, diet, nutrition, liver, kidney & bladder issues.

Price: $29.95 plus shipping & handling $5.95 (U.S. & Canada)

Canine Epilepsy: An Owner's Guide to Living With and Without Seizures

8.5" x 11" paperback, 194 pp,, illustrated, ISBN 0-9672253-3-7

Detailed discussions of nervous system function, seizure activity, medical, and alternative treatments, thyroid and liver disease. Includes an in-depth examination of seizure triggers, including diet, vaccines, and chemicals. Provides support for owners and instruction as how to assist dogs before, during, and after seizures.

Price: $29.95 plus shipping & handling $5.95 (U.S. & Canada)

And now on Video / DVD : *New Skills for Blind Dogs*

Call or visit our website for details on new videos/DVDs, package deals, placing credit card orders, and expedited shipping options. Orders are normally shipped within the U.S. via Postal service bookrate: a 5-8 day delivery. Canadian orders shipped via airmail. Make checks or money orders payable (in U.S. funds) to:

Lantern Publications
18709 S. Grasle Road
Oregon City, OR 97045-8899   USA

telephone & fax: **503-631-3491**
email: publisher@petcarebooks.com
website: **www.petcarebooks.com**